CW01065046

THINK LIKE AN
ACCOUNTANT

A non-accountant's guide to accounting.

Shubhasish Das, ACMA

THINK LIKE AN ACCOUNTANT

A non-accountant's guide to accounting

Shubhasish Das, ACMA

Dedicated to all my friends and colleagues who have inspired me to write this book

Copyright © 2018 Shubhasish Das

No part of this publication may be reproduced or distributed without express permission of the author.

Table of Contents

What is the purpose of this book?

The purpose of this book is to teach you how to think like an accountant. It will help you to:

- Understand the foundations of accounting

- Understand the thinking process Accountants follow to record transactions.

- Understand how Accountants prepare financial statements

What this book is not:

- This book is not a standard college text book. This **book builds your thinking process** so that you will find college text books easy to understand.

- The examples given in this book are conceptual in nature so that you will able be to grasp the basic concepts. I will build your **mindset** required for accounting. You need to practice the questions from your standard text book to get more grip on the concepts I discuss here.

What I promise:

- I promise you to make comfortable with the thinking process required for accounting so that you can understand advance accounting by yourself.

What I hope:

- I hope you will not underestimate the importance of the fundamentals of accounting. You will realize the importance of fundamentals in the advance stages of accounting.

- I hope you will be able to complete this mini book within a week and after reading this book you will have firm understanding of fundamentals.

- I hope after reading this book, your thick college text books looks less scary to you.

- I hope every non-accountant who is curious about accounting will get a good grasp of fundamentals of accounting.

Introduction

The universe is vast and complex. But it is made up of some elementary particles. And there are few basic laws which governs it. By understanding the interaction of these elementary particles and the basic laws of nature we can understand our physical universe.

Welcome to the accounting universe. The elementary particle of this universe is an **'account'**. The interaction between accounts gives birth to a vast and complex accounting universe. There are certain laws which governs it. These are called **accounting principles.**

An accountant is a scientist of accounting world. Scientists use scientific method to reach their conclusions. Likewise accountants use accounting methods. So are you ready to explore the accounting universe like an accountant?

I cannot cover the vastness and complexity of the accounting world within these few pages. But I will explain you the **structure and laws** upon which this universe is built.

This is what accounting does:

1. It records every transaction happening in the business. (Through Journal, Leger, and Trial balance. This part is also called **book keeping.**

2. It identifies the results of these transactions. (Through profit and loss statement/Income statement)

3. It identifies the financial position of your business. (Balance sheet)

4. It lets you know the cash flows through cash flow statement. (Out of the scope of this book)

This is what accounting is all about

1. Recording the transactions through Journal entries

2. Posting the journal entries to ledger accounts

3. Preparing the unadjusted trial balance.

4. Recording the adjustment entries.

4. Preparing adjusted trial balance

5. Closing the income and expenses accounts to profit and loss account

6. Preparing financial statements.

7. Interpreting the financial statements. (Out of scope of this book)

THINK LIKE AN ACCOUNTANT

Accountants' vocabulary

In order to understand the topics discussed in upcoming chapters you need to acquaint yourself with some of the basic terms of accounting. I will try to avoid accounting Jargon while explaining these terms.

Financial statements: Financial statements are end result of accounting. These includes Income statement, Balance sheet. Changes in owners' equity and cash flow statement.

Income statement: This is also called profit and loss statement. It contains all the incomes and expenses generated during an accounting period. The purpose of income statement is to identify profit or loss.

Balance sheet : This reflects financial position of a company at any point of time. It contains Assets, liabilities and owner's equity.

Assets: Assets are **resources** controlled by enterprise. These can be further classified as current and non-current assets.

Current assets: Cash and cash equivalents, assets which are expected to be converted into cash within the companies accounting cycle which is usually twelve months. *Example of current assets are inventories, accounts receivable, prepaid expanses etc.*

Non-Current assets : Any asset other than current asset is a non-current asset.

Example: Building, Goodwill, patent, long term investments

Fixed Assets: Fixed assets are property, plant and equipment which helps to carry out day to day business operations.

Example: Land, building, Machinery

Liability: These are amounts that business owes to lenders of funds.

Example: Accounts payable, debentures, Loans

Current liability: That portion of liability which is expected to be settled within next 12 months from the balance sheet date.

Example: Bank overdraft, Accounts payable, provision for taxation

Non-Current Liability: any liability other than current liability.

Example: Long term loans, debentures

Capital/ Owner's equity: This is the amount contributed by owners in the business.

Example: Equity share capital

Income: it is an inflow of economic benefits which results in the increase of owner's equity.

Example: income from sale of goods or provision of services, interest income etc.

Operating income: This is the income generated from the main activities of a business such as selling of goods or rendering of services.

Non-operating income: These are the incomes earned form activities other than the main activities of a business.

Examples: interest income, gain on sale of fixed assets.

Revenue: This is the income which business earns by selling goods or providing services.

Cost: Cost is an expenditure which can be either an asset or expense.

Expense: This a cost which is expired, used up or incurred to earn revenue. Expenses decrease Owners' equity.

Example: A building used for manufacturing is recorded at its cost as an asset. Depreciation provided for each accounting year is an expense.

Example: Good purchased are recorded as inventory under assets. When the goods sold, inventory is reduced and reported as expense called "cost of goods sold".

Example: Insurance paid in advance is $6000 for 6 months. This is an asset. However in each of the coming months this asset is reduced by 1000 and recognized as expense because it is expired.

Expenditure: It is a payment which may be for acquiring assets, reduction of liability (i.e.- repayment of loans), or expenses (i.e.-purchase of goods).

Revenue expenditure: It is a cost which is incurred to generate revenue. These are the costs which are used up or expensed in the period in which they occur.

Examples: cost of goods sold. Rent expenses

Capital expenditures: Cost which is incurred to acquire assets and includes costs which increases earning capacity of assets.

Operating expenses: These are the expenses related to day to day operations of business.

Non-operating expenses: Expenses which are not related to day to day operations of business. Loss or gain from sale of fixed assets.

Loss: Expenses which doesn't generate any income.

Reserves: Reserve is an appropriation of profit for a specific purpose.

Provisions: Provision is the estimated amount of expense recognized because of the unavailability of precise information.

CHAPTER 1 - BASICS

Chapter overview

1. General Ledger

2. Accounting equation

What is Business?

A. Business is a system.

B. it receives inputs, processes the inputs to produce goods and services.

C. it sales the goods and services to generate income. If income is more than the expenses, it makes profit. If expenses are more than income it generates loss.

Inputs	Process	Output	Result
Resourses	Manufacturing Trading	Goods/servises	Profit/loss

Every business does following set of **economic activities** (called **transactions**).

1. It acquires **assets.**

2. It raises **capital.** (From owners)

3. It incurs **liabilities.** (From Lenders)

4. It incurs **expenses**

5. It earns **incomes**

A simple model of business activities

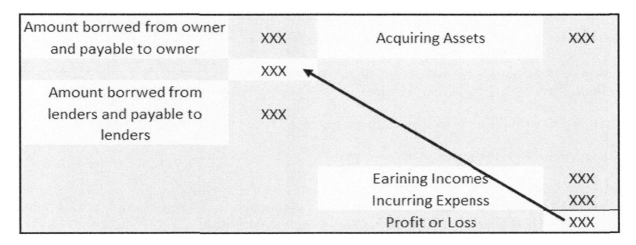

All the transactions in the business are some way or other falls under these activities or related to these activities. You may notice these activities can be captured under five categories: Assets, Liabilities, Capital, Income and expense. *These categories or headings are called accounts.*

Section 1 General Ledger

The basic element of accounting is an account. *Think of an account as a note book. You will have different notebooks to record different types of transactions. For example, all cash related transaction can be recorded in a notebook called cash account. To have clarity, you will record all the additions to the cash balance in one side and all the deductions from cash balance in other side. In this way you can track how the cash balance is increasing or decreasing and what is the net balance after a period.* And obviously you will record the transactions as they occur over a period of time in a chronological order. *Collectively all the accounts in a business is called* General **Ledger**.

A simple representation of an account is a T Account. It is called T account because it looks like T.

For example,

Cash Account

Cash account			
	Debit		Credit

The left side of an account is called Debit and the right side of an account is called credit. We will learn more about Debit and Credit in the next chapter.

One side of the account records additions (increases) to the account and other side records deductions (decreases) from the account.

The first step in accounting is to record the transactions occurring in the business.

1. Why recording of transactions is important?

The aim of accounting is to ascertain profit/loss and financial position of the business at the end of the period. Since every business transaction has an impact on the profit and loss and financial position, it is crucial that the transactions are recorded accurately.

2. The logical system for recording of transactions.

The whole system of accounting is based on the genius of one person's thinking. He is Luca Pacioli, the Italian mathematician, also known as the father of accounting.

How did he came up with this brilliant system?

If you are to think like him, following will be your observations:

Observation 1. Every business needs some resources to start. For example, you need a building, some cash, inventories etc. These resources are known as assets.

Observation 2. How do business acquire these resources? It is not a living entity right!. Somebody has given to it. Who? Either the owners or lenders.

This point is very subtle.

If you look deeper into what you have just observed, you will notice two very important things:

1. You thought of business as a 'separate entity' from owner. It can receive resources from owner and return resources to owner. Once you see it as separate from owner, it is obvious to you that it is separate from lenders too.

2. Every asset has an invisible 'claim' upon it. Who can have claim these assets? Obviously the owners and lenders.

Observation 3. Let's refine observation 2. It is helpful if you record the asset in the books and also record the claims upon it. It is clear that:

Claims = Assets. Let's give some name to the claims so that it is helpful for recording. Owner's claim on assets is called Capital. Lender's claim on assets is called liability.

Now you have converted your thoughts into a Mathematical formula:

Capital + Liability = Assets. This is called accounting equation. We will read more about accounting equation in next section.

Observation 4: Whatever economic activity (transactions) you do in the business, it is going to affect the assets and claims. What type of effect a transaction can have? It can either decrease the assets and claims or increase the assets and claims. If **total** assets increase, claim on these assets also increase by equal amount. If **total** assets decrease the claim on these assets on decrease by equal amount. Why I have used the word **"total"** ? Because assets in total is collection of many individual assets. It is possible that, in a transaction, an individual asset might increase and one or more individual asset may decrease by the same amount. In this case this transaction will not affect the Claims. Same can be thought of for the transactions within individual components of claims.

Observation 5: how all these observations are helpful? *It is helpful for one single reason.* **We have developed a mathematical equation.** And mathematics never lies. After the recording of every transaction: Capital + Liability must be equal to the Assets.

1. This gives us an assurance that what we have recorded in correct.

2. We can know what the business owns (Assets) and how much it owes to the owners (Capital) and Lenders (Liability) at any point of time.

I hope you have understood the logic behind the accounting system. We have different tools to record the transactions and ascertain the effect of transactions: General ledger, Journal, Trail balance, profit and loss account, and Balance sheet. We will know about these tools in later chapters but now you can see the logic which operates within all these tools.

2. How to record the transactions?

A. Think yourself as an accountant who represents business.

B. Think two sides of every transaction.

C. Record the transaction.

Let's take an example.

You are starting a business. You are investing $50000 cash.

This is your first transaction.

How to record this transaction?

A. **Think yourself as an accountant who represents business.** Although you are the owner of business, while recording the transactions you need to think from the angle of business.

B. **Think two sides of the transaction:** Since you represents business, you need to see the transaction from the perspective of business. What do you see?

1. Business is receiving money (Assets).

2. Business is borrowing the money from owner (you; represented by capital account)

You are able to see two sides of transaction right! ***This is the mindset you require to think like an accountant. You should always be able to see two sides of a transaction.***

3. The next thing you need to do is to record the transaction. You have already identified two sides of transaction. **These two sides of transaction are captured in two accounts.** In the above example, the two accounts are- Asset and Capital. There is a scientific way to record the transactions. It is called journal. *We will discuss more about Journal in a separate chapter.*

Cash account

Incresae	Decrease
50000	

Capital account

Decrease	Incresae
	50000

Note: *Since business is receiving cash, cash account is increased. Simultaneously business is borrowing this money from you (owner). So the capital account (which represents amount owed to owner) is also increased.*

Let's extend our example for few more transactions:

You borrowed $20000 from your friend to invest in the business.

How should you think about this transaction?

1. Business receives Cash of $20000.

2. Business is borrowing the cash from outsider (who is not the owner).

So the two sides of transaction are **receiving cash** and **borrowing cash**. Cash received is to be recorded in Cash account. Borrowing will be recorded in **Liability account**.

Cash account

Incresae	Decrease
20000	

Liability account

Decrease	Incresae
	20000

THINK LIKE AN ACCOUNTANT

Note: When business borrows cash, cash balance is increased. Simultaneously business is borrowing money from your friend which it needs to payback in future. Hence it will recognize an increase in liability too.

You purchase goods for $5000.

How should you think about this transaction?

1. Business incurs an expense of $5000 by purchasing goods.

2. Business pays cash of $5000.

So the two sides of transaction are incurring **expenses** and paying cash. Cash paid is to be recorded in Cash account. Expenses for purchase will be recorded in purchase account (Expense **account.**).

Cash Account

Incresae	Decrease
	5000

Expense account

Incresae	Decrease
5000	

Note: Paying cash will decrease the cash account balance and since expenses is incurred, expense account balance will increase.

You sold the goods for $6000.

How should you think about this transaction?

1. Business earns an income of $6000 by selling goods.

2. Business receives cash of $6000.

So the two sides of transaction are receiving **cash** and earning **income**. Cash received is to be recorded in Cash account. Income from sales will be recorded in sales account (Income **account**).

Icome account (sales account)

Incresae	Decrease
6000	

Cash account

Increase	Decrease
6000	

Note: Receiving cash will increase the cash account balance and selling of goods has generated income so income account is also increased.

Result of your transactions: you made a profit of $1000.

Summarize your expenses and losses in income statement (also called profit and loss statement).

Profit and loss statement

	Expenses		Incomes
Purchases	5000	Sales	6000
Balance(sales- purchases): profit	1000		
	6000		6000

Summarize your assets, liabilities and capital in Balance sheet (also called statement of financial position)

Balance sheet

	Capital + Liabilities		Assets
Capital (50000+1000)	51000	Cash	71000
Liability	20000	(50000+20000-5000+6000)	
	71000		71000

NOTE: *The profit of $1000 has formed part of capital. Why? Now think like an accountant. Business made a profit of $1000. To whom it obliges to repay the profit? Obviously it is the owner as he is the bearer of risk and return from the business.*

Important: From the previous example you have observed that there are actually five broad categories of Accounts namely: Assets, Liability, Capital, Income, and Expense. Everything in accounting is interaction between these five accounts. These are five basic elements of accounting universe.

(On a lighter note, it is like 5 infinity stones of Marvel universe)

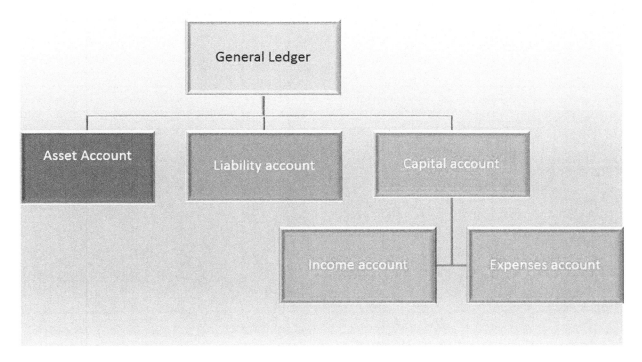

Chart of accounts

The first thing you want to do if you are starting an accounting system for your business is to prepare a chart of accounts. Chart of accounts is a **list of General Ledger accounts which is numbered in a systematic order.** Every GL account is identified by a number. It is very useful in computerized accounting system. You can write journal entries just using the account numbers.

Below is an **example** of chart of accounts

CHART OF ACCOUNTS of ABC Ltd.
General Ledger

ASSETS
1100 Cash
1200 Accounts Receivable
1300 Bills Receivable
1400 Inventory
1500 Office Supplies
1510 Store Supplies
1600 Prepaid Insurance
1700 Land
1800 Machineries
1810 Accumulated Depreciation- Machineries
1900 Building
1919 Accumulated Depreciation- Building

LIABILITIES

2100 Accounts Payable
2110 Salaries Payable
2120 Sales Tax Payable
2130 Bills Payable
2200 Long term loans

EQUITY/CAPITAL

3100 Capital or share capital
3110 Retained Earnings
3200 Dividends

REVENUE

4100 Sales
4200 Rent Revenue

EXPENSES

5100 Cost of Goods Sold
5200 Delivery Expense
5210 Advertising Expense
5220 Depreciation Expense-Store Equipment
5230 Depreciation Expense-Office Equipment
5250 Salaries Expense
5300 Rent Expense
5350 Insurance Expense
5400 Store Supplies Expense
5410 Office Supplies Expense
5450 Credit Card Expense
5500 Miscellaneous Expense
5600 Interest Expense

In the next section we will understand the relationship between the five categories of accounts.

Section 2 Relationship between five broad categories of Accounts—accounting equation

Do you remember the example from previous section? We have determined the financial position of your business.

	Balance sheet		
	Capital + Liabilities		Assets
Capital (50000+1000)	51000	Cash	71000
Liability	20000	(50000+20000-5000+6000)	
	71000		71000

The balance sheet or statement of financial position is a representation of what accountants call as accounting equation.

Capital + Liability = Assets

This is the basic form of accounting equation. At any point of time or after each transaction is recorded, the accounting equation must hold true (two side of accounting equation must be equal)

Let's add two more elements-incomes and expenses-to the equation. You know that incomes and expenses are summarized in profit or loss account to ascertain profit and loss. Ultimately profit or loss affects the owner's capital account.

Think of expenses are the resources spend from owner's capital and incomes are the resources added to owner's capital. Excess of income over expenses is profit and Excess of expenses over income is loss. Since it is not effective to adjust the owner's equity for every expenses and income, we record them separately in a statement: **Income statement or profit and loss account.** *The net result of profit and loss account is transferred to owner's equity; more discussion on profit and loss account in a separate chapter*

Revised Accounting equation: Asset = Liability + Capital + (Income – Expenses)

Or,

Assets + Expenses = Liability +Capital + Incomes

The left hand side of equation must be equal to the right hand side of equation after recording each transaction.

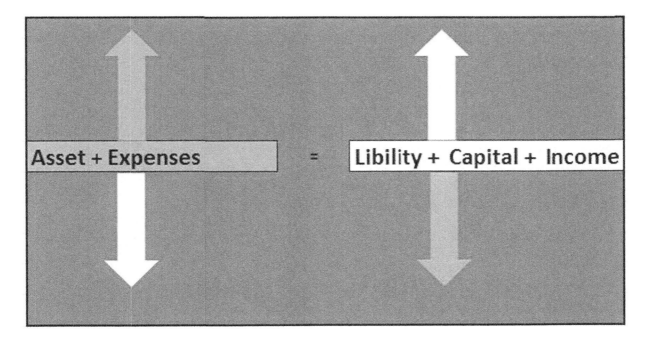

1. **Increase** *in the left side = Decrease in left side or increase in right side.*

*2. **Decrease** in the left side = Decrease in the right side or increase in the left side.*

*3. **Increase** in the right side = Increase in the left side or decrease in the right side.*

*4. **Decrease** in the right side = Decrease in the left side or increase in the right side.*

 It is important that you see the logic and the logic is: left side must be equal to right side after you adjust for increase and decrease in the accounts.

Summary

Now let us summarize what we have learned. In order to record a transaction we must have accountant's mindset. It is ***extremely important*** that you make yourself comfortable with this mindset.

Point 1. Accountant records all the transactions from the point of view of business. So while recording a transaction think yourself as an accountant.

Point 2. In every transaction, **at least** two accounts are involved. These two accounts represents two aspects of a transaction. There are only five broad categories of accounts. **You need to identify which accounts are involved in a transaction. You can use the below account identification matrix.**

Account idetification matrix

Account 1			Account 2		
	Asset	Expenses	Liability	Capital	Income
Asset					
Expenses					
Liability					
Capital					
Income					

Example: Rent paid $500.

Try to identify at least one account first. What is the first account come to notice? Rent account right! What is rent account? Rent is paid so Rent account is an expense. Congrats! You have identified the first account. Now look at the table and try to identify the 2nd account.

1. Is the other account income? We are not earning any income in this transaction.

2. Is the other account Capital? No capital account is involved in the transaction. We are not borrowing anything from owner.

3. is the other account a Liability? No liability is generated or settled in this transition. This is not a credit transaction.

4. Is the other account expenses. No, we have one expense account that we have already identified.

5. Is the other account Asset? **YES! What is the asset account that is involved? You see $500 is paid for rent right. Hence the other account is Cash.**

Account idetification matrix

Account 1		Account 2				
		Asset	Expenses	Liabiity	Capital	Income
Asset						
Expenses		YES	NO	NO	NO	NO
Liabiity						
Capital						
Income						

NOTE: This should be your ***thought process*** **while** identifying the account. In some transactions more than two accounts might be involved. You can apply same thought process to eliminate the account which are not involved in the transaction and identify the accounts which are involved in the transaction.

Point 3 Every transaction either increase or decrease the balance of the accounts involved. Note that a new account have starting balance as zero. So once you start recording transactions in an account you will either increase or decrease the balance. **You need to identify increases and decreases in the balance of accounts that are involved in a transaction.**

Example: continuing the previous example, Rent account balance will increase from $0 to $500. Cash account balance will decrease by $500

Point 4. Once you identified increases and decreases in the account, **you have to identify which side of account** you are going record the increases and decreases. *In the next chapter we will see how to identify which side of account you are going to record increases and decreases.*

Example. You know rent account balance is increasing and cash account balance is decreasing. Each of these accounts have two sides. Which side of rent account you should record the increase? Whether it should be left side or right side? Which side of cash account you should record decrease? We will see in the next chapter— **The Journal entry.**

CHAPTER 2 - THE JOURNAL ENTRY

Chapter overview

1. Journal

2 Posting to Ledger

Think of Journal as a record where the transactions are recorded for the first time.

This is how a traditional journal looks like. Note: in computerized environment you may not see this format. But this format is simple for visualization.

Date	Partiulars	Debit	Credit
1/1/2018	Accounts receivable a/c Dr. To Rent a/c Cr.	500	500
15/1/2018	Cash a/c Dr. To Accounts receivable a/c Cr.	500	500

Note: Account in short form is used as a/c. Dr. is the short form of Debit and Cr. is the short form of Credit.

You already know all the transactions in the accounting world are the interaction between five broad categories of accounts- Assets, liabilities, capital, incomes and expenses.

Journal is a method to record all these interactions in a systematic way. As discussed previously every account has a left side and right side. By convention, **Accountants call left hand side of an account Debit and right hand side credit.**

Account Balance: When amount in left side of an account is more than the right side of an account it is called **Debit balance.** When the amount in right side is more than the amount in left side it is called **credit balance.**

For example: below you can see the cash account. Debit side amount is $20000 and credit side $15000. Debit – Credit = $5000 debit balance remaining. We say cash account is having debit balance of $5000.

Cash account

Debit		Credit	
20000		15000	
	Balance	5000	
20000	Total	20000	

In the Loan account below, credit side amount is $20000 and debit side $13000. Credit - Debit = $7000 Credit balance remaining. We say Loan account is having a credit balance of $7000.

	Loan account		
	Debit		Credit
			20000
	13000		
Balance	**7000**		
	10000		10000

So, below are the basic questions we seek to answer through Journal.

What types of changes are possible in an account?

Answer:

1. Increase

2. Decrease

Which side of account I should record the increase or decrease?

Answer: Follow the rules of Journal entry (discussed later)

Through the accounting equation we can group the 5 broad accounts in two groups.

Asset + Expenses = Liability + Capital + Income

Group 1 = Asset and Expense

Group 2 = Liability, Capital and Income

Observation

A. These groups have **opposite nature**.

B. *Natural balance* of Group 1 accounts are debit balance. Natural balance of Group 2 accounts is Credit balance. *For easy remembering, we can say Group 1 accounts are **debit nature accounts** and Group 2 accounts are **credit nature accounts**.*

C. If we record increases in left side for Group 1, we should record increases for the Group 2 in the opposite side: right side. Whatever rule we follow for the first group, we should follow the opposite for the second group.

Rules of Journalizing

Below is the *convention (tradition)* which accountants follow to record the transactions: it is **called Modern approach or accounting equation approach**.

Increase in Asset and expense are recorded in debit side (left) and **decrease** is recorded in credit side. (Right)

Increase in Capital, Liability and Income are recorded in credit side (right) and **decrease** is recorded in debit side. (Left)

	Group 1 Assets + Expenses	Group 2 = Capital + Liabilities + Incomes
Increase	Debit	Credit
Decrease	Credit	Debit

This may be little difficult for you to remember now. But it will be very easy for you to visualize as you practice them in real situations.

How to think?

Increase in debit nature accounts are debited . *Decrease is credited.*

Increase in credit nature accounts are credited. *Decrease is debited.*

Just identify the nature of account-->increase is recorded in the same side as the nature of account-->decrease is recorded opposite side

Let us apply some creativity for your visualization of rules of debit and credit. You will find it much easier to grasp the rules of debit and credit once you are able to visualize them. Let's paint Journals.

Journal painting

Imagine you are painting a wall of your house. Left hand side of the wall you are painting in black and right hand side you are painting in white. Black represents debit nature accounts and white represents credit nature accounts.

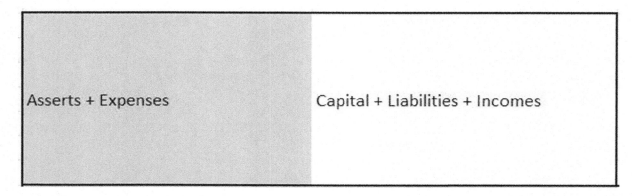

Visualize you have two paint brushes; one is black and other is white. **Let's call the black brush debit and white brush credit** . If you apply the black brush into black side of the wall it will *increase balckness* . **Debit increases the debit nature accounts.** If you apply black brush to the white side of the wall it will *decrease the whiteness*. **Debit decreases the credit nature accounts**. If you apply the white brush to the white side of the wall it will *increase the whiteness*. **Credit increases the credit nature accounts**. If you apply white brush into black side of the wall it will *decreases blackness* . **Credit decreases the debit nature accounts**.

Debit nature accounts (Black)		Credit nature accounts (White)	
Debit	Increase blanckness	Creidt	Increase whiteness
Creidt	Decrease Blackness	**Debit**	Decrease whiteness

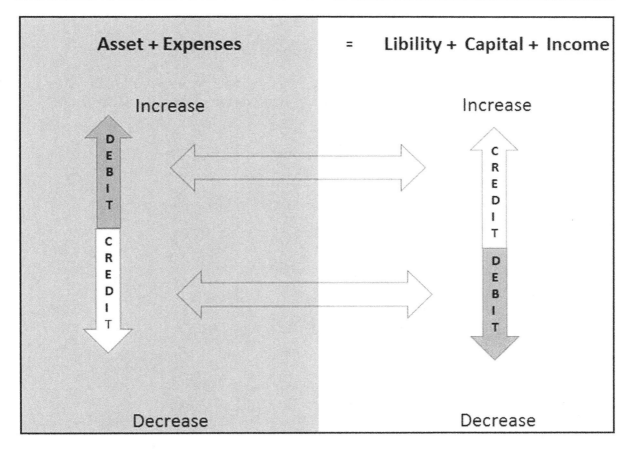

Note: There is another approach to record transactions which is called Traditional approach. I don't recommend the use of traditional approach as you will find it difficult to record the transactions in advance stages of accounting and it will create a lot of confusion. I have observed many students even professionals struggling with advance entries because their mindset is used to this approach. But just for the sake of completeness of the discussion, I am including the method below.

Traditional Approach:

Accounts are divided in three groups: Personal, Nominal and Real. The classification of accounts are helpful. But the rules for debit and credit will not be very helpful in advance accounting.

Personal accounts: Debtors and creditors

Real accounts: Assets

Nominal accounts: Incomes and Expenses

Rule:

Personal accounts: Debit the receiver and credit the giver

Real accounts: Debit what comes in and credit what goes out

Nominal account: Debit all expenses and losses, and credit all incomes and gains

I strictly recommend not to follow traditional approach and if you are following it currently, forget it and start to think like an accountant with modern approach! You will not be disappointed.

So let's forget about traditional approach and go through few examples to see how we can use the Accounting equation approach in practical situations.

I will try to classify all the journal entries that are possible into below groups:

1. Entries involving cash

2. Entries related credit purchase of goods or services.

3. Entries related to credit sale of goods or services.

4. Entries related to expenses and losses

5. Entries related to Incomes and gains

6. Accrual and adjustment entries

7. Transfer entries.

8. Opening entries

9. Closing entries.

10. Miscellaneous entries.

We will also see how these entries will be posted to General Ledger

Note: there can be infinite type of entries. **But remember all entries are limited to five broad accounts. I promise**, once you understand the logic I am discussing in this book, there is **no** entry in the universe you cannot comprehend and record. Just understand the logic and mindset from my book and take any standard college text book to practice or if you are a working accountant, try to apply the concepts discussed here to your practical work.

Thinking Tip:

A. Journal recording process

There are four step thinking process for recording any journal entry.

Step 1: *Always think yourself as an accountant who represents business. Record the transactions from the perspective of business.*

Step 2: *Identify the two or more accounts involved. Initially it is helpful if you use account identification matrix. After one month of practice you will be able see the accounts that are involved easily without the help of matrix.*

Step 3: *Identify the increase and decrease in the accounts involved.*

Step 4: *follow the modern approach to record the transaction.*

B. posting to ledger

1. Open general ledger accounts for each of the accounts involved the transaction.

2. Record the debit side entries starting with 'To'

3. Record the credit side entries starting with 'By'

4. Record an opening debit balance with "To balance b/d (brought down)

5. Record an opening credit balance with "By balance b/d (brought down)

6. Record a Closing debit balance with "By balance c/d (carried down)

7. Record a Closing credit balance use "To balance c/d (carried down)

Opening balance means balance brought down from previous period.

Closing balance means balance to be carried down to next period.

*These are the **conventional notation** accountants follow. You may not see these in the computerized environment.*

I. Entries transactions involving cash.

These are the transactions which involves cash receipt or payment. Some examples are below

1. You have started a company called ABC limited with a capital of $30000.

*How to record this transaction **in the books of ABC limited**?*

A. Accounts involved in the transaction: Cash and Capital.

B. Cash is asset and Capital is owner's contribution.

C. There is increase in Cash account and increase in the Capital account.

D. Increase in asset is debited and increase in capital is credited. (Remember the logic: increase in debit nature accounts are debited and increase in credit nature accounts are credited)

Date	Partiulars	Debit	Credit
12/9/2017	Cash a/c debited	30000	
	To Capital a/c credited		30000

Cash account

	Debit		Credit
To balance b/d	NIL		
To Capital a/c	30000		
	30000	Total	30000

Capital account

	Debit		Credit
		By balance b/d	NIL
		By cash a/c	30000
	30000	Total	30000

2. A ltd. Purchases a building worth $5000.

A. Accounts involved in the transaction: Cash and Building.

B. Cash and Building both are assets.

C. There is increase in Building account and decrease in the Cash account.

D. Increase in asset is debited and decrease in asset is credited. (Remember the logic: increase in debit nature accounts are debited and decrease in debit nature accounts are credited)

Date	Partiulars	Debit	Credit
22/9/2017	building a/c debited	5000	
	To cash a/c credited		5000

Building account

	Debit		Credit
To balance b/d	NIL		
To cash a/c	5000		
		By balance c/d	5000
	5000	Total	5000

Cash account

	Debit		Credit
To balance b/d	NIL	By Building a/c	5000
To Capital a/c	30000		
		By balance c/d	25000
	30000		30000

3. A ltd. taken a loan of $3000.

A. Accounts involved in the transaction: Loan and cash

B. Loan is a liability and cash is an asset

C. There is an increase in Loan account and increase in cash account.

D. Increase in asset is debited and increase in Liability is credited. (Remember the logic: increase in debit nature accounts are debited and increase in credit nature accounts are credited)

Date	Partiulars	Debit	Credit
22/9/2017	Cash a/c debited	3000	
	To Loan a/c credited		3000

Loan Account

	Debit			Credit
		By balance b/d		NIL
		By Cash a/c		3000
To balance c/d	3000			
	3000	Total		3000

Cash account

	Debit		Credit
To balance b/d	NIL	By Building a/c	5000
To Capital a/c	30000		
To Loan a/c	3000		
		By balance c/d	28000
	33000		33000

4. Goods worth $2000 purchased in cash

A. Accounts involved in the transaction: Purchase and cash

B. Purchase is an expenses and Cash is an asset

C. There is an increase in purchase and decrease in cash.

D. Increase in expenses are debited and decrease in assets are credited. (Remember the rule: increase in debit nature accounts are debited and decrease in debit nature accounts are credited)

Date	Partiulars	Debit	Credit
22/9/2017	Purchases a/c debited	2000	
	To Cash a/c credited		2000

Purchases account

	Debit		Credit
To balance b/d **(Note 1)**	NA		
To Cash	2000		
		By profit and loss account **(Note 2)**	
	2000	Total	2000

Cash account

	Debit		Credit
To balance b/d	NIL	By Building a/c	5000
To Capital a/c	30000	By Purchases	2000
To Loan a/c	3000		
		By balance c/d	26000
	33000		33000

NOTE 1: Income and expenses accounts (also called nominal accounts) never carried to next period. So there will not be any opening balance for these accounts.

NOTE 2. We transfer all the income and expenses account to profit and loss account (also called income statement) at the end of the accounting period.

5. Goods worth $3000 sold in cash

A. Accounts involved in the transaction: Sales and cash

B. Sales is an Income and Cash is asset

C. There is an increase in sales and increase in cash.

D. Increase in income is credited and increase in asset is debited. (Remember the logic: increase in credit nature accounts are credited and increase in debit nature accounts are debited)

Date	Partiulars	Debit	Credit
28/9/2017	cash a/c debited	3000	
	To Sales a/c credited		3000

Sales account

Debit			Credit
		By balance b/d (Note 1)	NA
		By Cash	3000
To profit and loss account (Note 2)	3000		
	3000	Total	3000

Cash account

Debit			Credit
To balance b/d	NIL	By Building a/c	5000
To Capital a/c	30000	By Purchases	2000
To Loan a/c	3000		
To sales a/c	3000		
		By balance c/d	29000
	36000		33000

NOTE 1: Income and expenses accounts (also called nominal accounts) never carried to next period. So there will not be any opening balance for these accounts.

NOTE 2. We transfer all the income and expenses account to profit and loss account (also called income statement) at the end of the accounting period.

6. Salaries paid $500

A. Accounts involved in the transaction: Salaries and cash

B. Salaries is an Expense and Cash is asset

C. There is an increase in Salaries and decrease in cash.

D. Increase in expenses are debited, decrease in asset is credited. (Remember the logic: increase in debit nature accounts are debited and decrease in debit nature accounts are credited)

Date	Partiulars	Debit	Credit
28/9/2017	Salaries a/c debited	500	
	To Cash a/c credited		500

Salaries account

	Debit		Credit
To balance b/d **(Note 1)**	NA		
To Cash	500		
		By profit and loss account **(Note 2)**	500
	500	Total	500

Cash account

	Debit		Credit
To balance b/d	NIL	By Building a/c	5000
To Capital a/c	30000	By Purchases	2000
To Loan a/c	3000	By Salaries	500
To sales a/c	3000		
		By balance c/d	28500
	36000		36000

NOTE 1: Income and expenses accounts (also called nominal accounts) never carried to next period. So there will not be any opening balance for these accounts.

NOTE 2. We transfer all the income and expenses account to profit and loss account (also called income statement) at the end of the accounting period.

Before we proceed further let me introduce the concept of contra accounts

Contra accounts:

These accounts are used to ***reduce the balance*** of a related account. These accounts are paired with their related accounts while reporting in financial statements. These accounts will have the *opposite balance* of their related account. So the rules of debit and credit is **exactly opposite** for the contra accounts.

The reason for maintaining contra accounts rather than directly reducing the related account is to track the original balance of the account.

Nature of contra asset account is same as nature of liabilities for the purpose of recording.

Nature of contra liability account is same as nature of assets for the purpose of recording.

Increase in **Contra** Asset and expense are recorded in credit side and decrease recorded in debit side.

Increase in **Contra** Capital, Liability and Income are recorded in debit side and decrease is recorded in credit side.

	Contra Assets/Expenses	Contra Capital/Liabilities/Incomes
Increase	Credit	Debit
Decrease	Debit	Credit

II. Entries related to credit purchase of goods and services.

1. Goods purchase on credit $2500

A. Accounts involved in the transaction: purchase and accounts payable.

B. Purchase is an expense and Accounts payable is liability.

C. There is an increase in purchase and increase in accounts payable.

D. Increase in expenses is debited and increase in liabilities is credited. (Remember the logic: increase in debit nature accounts are debited and increase in credit nature accounts are credited)

Date	Partiulars	Debit	Credit
28/9/2017	Purchases a/c debited	2500	
	To Accounts payable a/c credited		2500

Purchases account

	Debit		Credit
To balance b/d **(Note 1)**	NA		
To Accounts payable	2500		
		By profit and loss account **(Note 2)**	500
	2500	Total	2500

Accounts payable

	Debit		Credit
		By Balance b/d	NIL
		By purchases	2500
To balance c/d	2500		
	2500		2500

Note 1. Since it is a expense account, it will be closed to profit and loss account.

2. Good returned to the vendor worth $500.

THINK LIKE AN ACCOUNTANT

A. Accounts involved in the transaction: purchase return and accounts payable.

B. Purchase return is a **contra expense account (as it is reducing the balance of purchases)** and Accounts payable is liability.

C. There is an increase in purchase return and decrease in accounts payable.

D. Increase in the contra expense account is credited and decrease in liability is debited. (Remember the rule: increase in credit nature accounts are credited-for the purpose of recording contra expense account is a credit nature account- and decrease in credit nature accounts are debited)

Date	Partiulars	Debit	Credit
10/10/2017	Accounts payable a/c debited	500	
	To purchase return a/c credited		500

Purchase return account

	Debit			Credit
		By balance b/d **(Note 1)**		NA
		By Accounts payable		500
To profit and loss account **(Note 2)**	500			
	500	Total		500

Accounts payable

	Debit			Credit
		By Balance b/d		NIL
To purchase return	500	By purchases		2500
To balance c/d	2000			
	2500			2500

NOTE 1: Contra income and expenses account balances will not be carried forward to next period. So there will not be any opening balance for these accounts.

NOTE 2. We transfer contra income and expenses account balances to profit and loss account. These accounts will be paired with their related accounts in the profit and loss account or income statement.

Income statement	Amount
Cash purchases	2000
Credit purchasses	2500
Less: Purchase return	500
Net purchases	4000

Note: *whenever goods are returned to vendor, a document is sent to the vendor notifying the same. It is called* **debit note** *. It is named as debit note because we are debiting the vendor account (decreasing the vendor account).*

Below is a sample debit note issued by ABC ltd for goods returned to XYZ ltd.

	ABC Limited Xaviar street No-117 **DEBIT NOTE**	Date: 15/12/2017
Against: XYZ Limited Peters Road		
Goods Returned as per delivery Challan no:95		$500
		Manager Lance Howard

o3. Paid to vendor $1700 in full settlement of his credit.

Amount due to vendor was 2500. Goods returned to vendor was $500. So amount due to the vendor is 2000. Amount paid to settle the balance is $1700. So discount received = 2000 – 1700 = 300

A. Accounts involved in this transaction: accounts payable, cash, discount received.

B. Discount received is an income, cash is an asset and accounts payable is a liability.

C. There is a decrease in accounts payable, decrease in cash and increase in discount received.

D. Decrease in liability is debited, decrease in asset is credited and increase in income is credited.

Date	Partiulars	Debit	Credit
15/10/1900	Accounts payable a/c debited To Cash a/c credited To Disount received a/c credited	2000	1700 300

Accounts Payabe accaunt

	Debit		Credit
		By balance b/d	Nil
To purchase return	500	By Puechases	2500
To Cash	1700		
To Discount Received	300		
	2500	Total	2500

Cash account

	Debit		Credit
To balance b/d	NIL	By Building a/c	5000
To Capital a/c	30000	By Purchases	2000
To Loan a/c	3000	By Salaries a/c	500
To sales a/c	3000	By Accounts payable a/c	1700
		By balance c/d	26800
	36000		36000

Discount received account

	Debit		Credit
		By Balance b/d	NA
		BY Accounts payable a/c	300
To profit and loss account			
	300	Total	300

The above entry is called a **compound entry** as it is combination of two entries.

Note: Subsidiary Ledger for Accounts payable and purchase returns

Due to large number of transaction for credit purchases, big companies maintain **sub ledgers** for credit purchases and purchase return.

A sub ledger for credit purchases contain name of the vendor, quantity and price of good purchased and the date on which it is purchased.

Similarly a sub ledger for purchase return record all the details relating quantity and price of goods returned.

These sub ledgers are totaled at periodic intervals and the total balance is transferred to purchase account and purchase returns account

III. Entries related to credit sale of goods.

1. Goods sold on credit $2000

A. Accounts involved in the transaction: sales and accounts receivable.

B. Sales is an income and Accounts receivable is an asset.

C. There is an increase in sales and increase in accounts receivable.

D. Increase in income is credited and increase in asset is debited. (Remember the logic: increase in credit nature accounts are credited and increase in debit nature accounts are debited)

Date	Partiulars	Debit	Credit
25/10/2017	Accounts receivable a/c debited	3000	
	To sales a/c credited		3000

Accounts Receivable account

	Debit		Credit
To balance b/d	NIL		
To Sales	3000		
		By balance c/d	3000
	3000	Total	3000

Sales account

	Debit		Credit
		By balance b/d	NA
		By Accounts receivable	3000
To profit and loss account	3000		
	3000	Total	3000

2. Good returned by the customer worth $500.

A. Accounts involved in the transaction: Sales return and Accounts receivable.

B. Sales return is a **contra income** Accounts receivable is Asset *For the purpose of recording think of contra income as a debit nature account.*

C. There is an increase in Sales return and decrease in accounts Receivable.

D. Increase in contra income is debited and decrease in asset is credited. (Remember the rule: increase in debit nature accounts are debited and decrease in debit nature accounts are debited)

Date	Partiulars	Debit	Credit
25/10/2017	Sales Return a/c debited	500	
	To Accounts Receivable a/c credited		500

Accounts Receivable account

	Debit		Credit
To balance b/d	NIL		
To Sales	3000	By Sales Return	500
		By balance c/d	2500
	3000	Total	3000

Sales Return account

	Debit		Credit
To balance b/d	NA		
To Accounts receivable	500		
		By profit and loss account	500
	500	Total	500

NOTE 1: Contra income and expenses account balances will not be carried forward to next period. So there will not be any opening balance for these accounts.

NOTE 2. We transfer contra income and expenses account balances to profit and loss account. These accounts will be paired with their related accounts in the profit and loss account or income statement.

Since sales return is a contra account, it shall be paired with sales account while reporting in Income statement.

Income statement	Amount
Cash Sales	3000
Credit Sales	3000
Less: Sales return	500
Net Sales	5500

*Note: whenever goods are returned from customer, a document is sent to the customer notifying the same. It is called **Credit note**. It is named as credit note because we are crediting (decreasing) the customer account (Asset).*

Below is a sample of credit note issued by ABC ltd for Good received from XYZ ltd.

	ABC Limited Xaviar street No-117	Date: 15/12/2017
	CREDIT NOTE	
Against: XYZ Limited Peters Road		
Goods Received as per delivery Challan no:95		$500
		Manager Lance Howard

3. Received from customer $2300 in full settlement for his credit.

Amount due from customer was $3000. Goods returned from customer was $500. Net amount due from customer was 2500. Amount received from customer in full settlement is 2300. Discount given to customer is 2500-2300 = 200.

A. Accounts involved in the transaction: accounts receivable, cash, discount given.

B. Cash is an asset, accounts receivable is an asset and discount given is an Expense.

C. There is an increase in Cash, decrease in Accounts receivable and increase in discount paid.

D. increase in assets and expenses are debited, decrease in assets are credited. (Remember the logic: increase in debit nature accounts are debited and decrease in debit nature accounts are credited)

Date	Partiulars	Debit	Credit
15/10/2017	Cash a/c debited	2300	
	Discount paid a/c credited	200	
	Accounts receivable a/c credited		2500

Accounts receivable account

	Debit		Credit
To balance b/d	NIL		
To Sales	3000	By Sales return	500
		By Discount paid	200
		By Cash	2300
		By Balance c/d	NIL
	3000	Total	3000

Cash account

	Debit		Credit
To balance b/d	NIL	By Building a/c	5000
To Capital a/c	30000	By Purchases	2000
To Loan a/c	3000	By Salaries	500
To sales a/c	3000	By Accoiunts payable	1700
To Accounts receivable	2300		
		By balance c/d	29100
	38300		38300

Discount paid account

	Debit		Credit
To balance b/d	NIL		
To Accounts recevable a/c	200	By profit and loss a/c	200
	200		200

The above entry is called a **compound entry** as it is combination of two entries.

Note: Subsidiary Ledger for Accounts receivable and Sales returns

Due to large number of transaction for credit sales, big companies maintain **sub ledgers** for credit sales and sales return.

A sub ledger for credit sales contain name of the customer, quantity and price of good sold and the date on which it is sold.

Similarly a sub ledger for sales return record all the details relating quantity and price of goods returned.

These sub ledgers are totaled at periodic intervals and the total balance is transferred to sales account and sales return account.

IV. Entries related to expenses and losses

1. Administrative/sales/distribution expenses paid.

A. Accounts involved are: Expenses account, Cash account or payable a/c

B. Increase in expenses is debit, decrease in cash is credit. Increase in payable (liability is credit).

Date	Partiulars	Debit	Credit
XX/XX/XXXX	Respective Expenses account	XXX	
	To Cash a/c **or** payable a/c credited		XXX

2. Building carrying a book value of $5000, sold at 4500.

A. Accounts involved in the transaction: fixed asset, cash, loss on sale of fixed assets.

B. There is an increase in cash, decrease in fixed asset and increase in loss.

C. Increase in asset and expenses is debited, decrease in asset is credited. (Remember the logic: increase in debit nature accounts are debited and decrease in debit nature accounts are credited)

Date	Partiulars	Debit	Credit
15/11/2017	Cash a/c debited	4500	
	Loss on sale of fixed assets	500	
	Building a/c credited		5000

Building a/c

	Debit		Credit
To balance b/d	NIL		
To Cash	5000	By Cash	4500
		By Loss on sale of fixed assets	500
		By Balance c/d	NIL
	5000	Total	5000

Cash account

	Debit		Credit
To balance b/d	NIL	By Building a/c	5000
To Capital a/c	30000	By Purchases	2000
To Loan a/c	3000	By Salaries	500
To sales a/c	3000	By Accoiunts payable	1700
To Accounts receivable	2300		
To Fixed assets a/c	4500	By balance c/d	33600
	42800		42800

Loss on sale of fixed assets account

	Debit		Credit
To balance b/d	NA		
To Fixed assets a/c	500	By profit and loss a/c	500
	500		500

V. Entries related to incomes and gains.

A. Accounts involved are: incomes/gains account, Cash account or receivable a/c

B. Increase in incomes/gains is credit, increase in cash is debit, and Increase in receivable is debit.

44

Date	Partiulars	Debit	Credit
XX/XX/XXXX	Cash or Recivable a/c debited	XXX	
	To respective incomes or gains a/c credited		XXX

NOTE: After reading until this, you should have started seeing the significance of Journal and ledger. Suppose you want to see how much cash balance you have now in the business. You can easily know it by looking at the cash account.

VI. Accrual and adjustment entries

Please refer to the chapter **adjustment entries.**

VII. Transfer entries.

Sometimes we need to transfer the balance from one account to other account. These entries are called transfer entries.

The account from which balance is transferred = decrease

The account to which it is transferred = increase (if same nature balance received), **decrease** (if opposite nature balance received)

Example: A Ltd. is maintaining two bank accounts; wells Fargo and Citibank. Money transferred from Citibank account to Wells Fargo account.

A. Accounts involved in the transaction. Wells Fargo a/c and Citi bank a/c

B. Both are assets.

C. Well Fargo balance is decreasing and Citibank balance is increasing

Debit: City Bank a/c (it is a debit nature account and receiving debit balance-increase in balance)

Credit: Well Fargo bank a/c (decrease in asset account debited).

The easy way is to write the entry is to reverse the account from which the balance is transferred and offset the transferee account with opposite balance. Though I recommend to understand the logic described above.

1. From which account balance is transferred?—Wells Fargo

2. What type of balance is transferred?—debit balance

3. Reverse the Wells Fargo account—Wells Fargo account is credited.

4. What the account receiving the balance?—City bank

5. How can you complete the entry?—Debit city bank account.

Date	Partiulars	Debit	Credit
XX/XX/XXXX	City Bank account	XXX	
	Wells Fargo account		XXX

Transferring entries are very common. All the incomes/gains and expenses and losses are **transferred** to profit and loss account (Income statement) at the end of accounting period.

Note that profit and loss account is a credit nature account as the net balance of this account is part of owner's equity.

You should also understand that debit nature accounts doesn't mean they must have debit balance and credit nature accounts doesn't mean they must have credit balance . Through profit and loss account is a credit nature account it can have net balance as loss (debit balance). Another example is, accounts receivable is a debit nature account, but if it shows a credit balance it may be that we received an advance from customer. **While recording journals our focus should be the nature of accounts; which we have discussed in detail previously.**

VIII. Opening entries

Opening entries are recorded to bring previous periods' asset and liability into the current period books.

Suppose you have another business B ltd. you have started last year. Below are the assets, liabilities and capital balance. You need to transfer these balances to current year books. The entry you will pass is called opening entry.

Balance sheet of B Ltd. As on 31-12-2016			
Equity and liabilities	$	Assets	$
Capital	10000	Building	10000
Reserves	5000	Machinary	7000
		investments	3000
Long term loans	10000	Accounts receivable	2000
Accounts payable	3000	Inventories	3000
provsions	2000	Cash	5000
	30000		30000

Record the opening entry for 1-1-2017.

Debit all the debit nature accounts and credit all the credit nature accounts.

Date	Partiulars	Debit	Credit
1/1/2018	Building a/c debited	10000	
	Machinary a/c debited	7000	
	Investment a/c debited	3000	
	Accounts receivable a/c debited	2000	
	Inventories a/c debited	3000	
	Cash a/c debited	5000	
	Capital a/c credited		10000
	Reserves a/c credited		5000
	Long term loans a/c credited		10000
	Accounts payable a/c credited		3000
	provsions a/c credited		2000

Posting to leader: Let's take two examples: building account and Capital account. Posting to other accounts will follow similar logic.

Building a/c

	Debit		Credit
To balance b/d	10000		
	10000		10000

Capital a/c

	Debit		Credit
		By balance b/d	10000
	10000		10000

IX. Closing entries: Please refer the chapter "Income statement"

X. Miscellaneous entries.

Any entry which is not covered under above categories.

1. A ltd. had taken a loan of $10000. It could not pay the loan. The bank agreed to take the Land owned by A ltd. which has a realizable value of $10000.

A. Accounts involved in the transaction: Loan from Bank a/c and Land a/c

B. Loan is a liability and Land is an asset.

B. There is a decrease in Loan a/c and decrease in Land a/c

C. Decrease in liability is debited and decrease in asset is credited. (Remember the logic: decrease in credit nature accounts are debited and decrease in debit nature accounts are credited)

Date	Partiulars	Debit	Credit
15/12/2017	Loan a/c debited	10000	
	Land a/c Credited		10000

2. Owner withdraws cash for personal use.

A. Accounts involved in this transaction: Cash a/c and Drawings a/c

B. Cash a/c is an asset and Drawings a/c is a Contra Capital a/c

C. There is an increase in Contra Capital a/c and decrease in Cash a/c.

D. Increase in Contra Capital account is debited and decrease in Asset account is credited. . (Remember the logic: increase in debit nature accounts are debited-for the purpose of recording, contra capital a/c is considered as debit nature a/c- and decrease in debit nature accounts are credited)

Note

1. Withdrawal of cash or goods by owner for his personal use is reduced from Capital account.

2. For the purpose of reducing the Capital account we use Drawings a/c.

3. Drawings account is **not** an expenses for Business hence it will not be transferred to profit and loss account.

Date		Partiulars	Debit	Credit
15/12/2017		Drowings a/c debited	10000	
		Cash a/c Credited		10000

Balance Sheet				
Equuity and liability				**Assets**
Capital	XXX			
Less: Drowings	10000			

CHAPTER 3 - THE PRINCIPLES OF ACCOUNTING WORLD

There are certain principles which guide accountants in recording of business transactions. Summary of accounting principles:

1. Principles related to Assets and liabilities

- Going concern

- Historical cost

2. Principles related to Incomes and expenses

- Accrual

- Matching

- Conservatism

3. Principles related to Owner's equity.

- Business entity concept

4. Principles related to overall preparation and presentation of financial statements.

- Monetary unit

- Periodicity

- Consistency

- Materiality

Note: You may find it difficult to understand the contents of this section at one go. So I will discuss only the principles related to incomes and expenses—Accrual, matching and conservatism now so that you can understand the chapter Adjusting entries. I am adding other concepts in the Appendix 1. You should refer to the Appendix 1 time and time again after reading other chapters. You should be able to see the underlying principle behind the recording of every business transaction.

Principles related to Incomes and expenses

Accrual Principle

There are two types of accounting system.

Cash system of accounting: This system of accounting is followed in small businesses. In this system expenses are recorded *when they are **paid in cash*** and incomes are recorded *when they are **received in cash***.

Example: You have paid three months advance rent amounting $3000 in October 2017. What is amount for rent expenses you will be reporting in your October books?

If you are maintaining books as per cash system, you will record $3000 as rent expense. Because of this the cash you have paid in October for rent.

Accrual system of accounting: This accounting system is governed by accrual principle.

As per this system, revenues are recorded when they are ***earned*** not when they are received in cash and expenses are recorded when they are ***incurred*** not when they are paid in cash.

How to think?

Point 1: Identify the incomes and expenses.

Point 2: Identify the period in which they were earned or incurred.

Point 3: Record the incomes and expenses in that period.

Example:

1. Alex sold goods in January but the money has been received in February

- *Identify the income: Revenue from sales.*

- *Identify the period in which it is earned: The sales is completed in January. So the period in which the revenue is earned is January.*

- *Record the revenue income in January.*

2. Alex paid rent for January in February.

- *Identify the expenses: Rent.*

- *Identify the period in which it is incurred: Rent is due in January and it is related to January.*

- *Record Rent expenses in January.*

Accrual concept is one of the fundamental concepts of accounting. Almost all the companies all over the world maintain accrual accounting system. ***So it is very important for you to understand this concept once and for all.***

Due to accrual concept we shall be dealing with below types of transactions:

- Expenses due but not paid: Expenses payable/accrued/outstanding

- Prepaid expenses: Expenses paid in advance.

- Incomes earned but not received: Accrued income.

- Unearned income: Income received in advance.

   You will learn more about how to record these transactions in chapter Adjusting Entries

Matching Principle

This concept is about **when to recognize the expenses in profit and loss account.** Expenses should be recognized at the same period in which corresponding revenue or benefit is recognized. This way expenses will be matched with incomes they help to generate.

How to think?

Point 1. Identify the expenses which is incurred to generate a specific income.

Point 2: Identify the period in which the income is recognized.

Point 3: Record the expenses in the same period in which the income is recognized

Note: There are some expenses for which corresponding revenue cannot be identified. They are related to specific period. For example, rent, depreciation, salary of the office staff, electricity bill. **These expenses are recorded as per accrual concept.**

Example: A ltd. is a trading company which buys goods from wholesalers and sells in retail. It brought 100 units at $5 in January. It sold 80 units in February at $6. When the expenses for goods purchased will be recorded and how much?

- *Identify the expenses: cost of purchase of goods.*

- *Identify the period in which the revenue is recognized: Revenue for 80 units of goods recognized in February. Since 20 units is still not sold, for these revenue is not recognized in February.*

- *Record the expenses in the same period in which the revenue is recognized: Cost for 80 units of goods **has to be recognized as expense** in profit and loss a/c in February as corresponding income from these units are recognized in February. So the total expenses* *recognized in February is 80 units * $5 = $400. Cost of remaining 20 units which are unsold will be recorded as closing stock and carried to the balance sheet.*

Note: Although the cost incurred in January is 100 units * $5 = $500 no expenses will be recognized in the profit and loss account in January. Only in February the expenses of $400 will be recognized to match the revenue.

Conservatism principle

This principles tells us to follow a conservative approach while recording incomes and profits. You should **record possible losses** but should **not** record possible gains. This prevents overstating the financial position of the company. When present with alternatives, an accountant should chose the alternative resulting in high loss & less income and less asset value & more liability amount.

Example: you brought inventories at a cost of $10000 before six months. These inventories could not be sold during the year and still in stock. The present market value of these inventories are $9000. You need to spend extra $1000 on packing. You are going to prepare the financial statements. What is the value of inventory you should be reporting in your financial statement?

A) Recognize the inventories at $10000 and ignore the loss of $1000 due to decline of market value.

*B) Recognize the inventory at **net realizable value** (market value **less** amount needs to be spent to complete the sale: $9000-$1000 = $8000) and recognize the loss of $2000 (cost of purchase $10000 less net realizable value $8000) in income statement due to decline in the value of inventory and cost to complete the sale.*

As per the conservative principle, the accountant should follow option B.

CHAPTER 4 - TRIAL BALANCE

As we already know general ledgers will either have a debit balance or credit balance. Trial balance is nothing but a **summary** of closing debit and credit balances of accounts.

The accounting equation tells us that all the debits should be equal to the credits. This is why debit balance in trial balance should equal to the credit balance. If they are not equal, then there must be some error while recording the transaction.

Example: *A ltd. has following balances as on 31-12-2017. Prepare a trial balance for A ltd.*

Credit balances: Capital a/c $20000, Long term Loans a/c $9000, Accounts payable a/c $5000, Short term Loans a/c $7000, Gain from sale of fixed assets a/c $4500, interest income a/c $300, Sales a/c $5000.

Debit balances: Building a/c $10000, Machinery a/c $6000, Investments a/c $1000, Land a/c $4000, Furniture a/c 2000, Accounts receivable a/c 4000, Cash a/c $8000, Bank $6000, Advertisement expenses a/c $5000, Rent a/c 800, purchases a/c 3000, Salaries a/c 1000.

Prepare the trial balance in below format

Trial balance as on 31-12-2017

Particulars (Ledger a/c ending balances)	Debit ($)	Credit ($)
Captial		20,000.00
Long term loans		9,000.00
Accounts payable		5,000.00
Short term loans		7,000.00
Building	10,000.00	
Machinary	6,000.00	
Investments	1,000.00	
Land	4,000.00	
Furniture	2,000.00	
Accounts receivable	4,000.00	
Cash	8,000.00	
Bank	6,000.00	
Purchases	3,000.00	
Salaries	1,000.00	
Rent	800.00	
Advertisiing expenses	5,000.00	
Gain from sale of Fixed assets		4,500.00
Interest income		300.00
Sales		5,000.00
Total	50,800.00	50,800.00

The primary purpose behind preparing trial balance is to check if there is any error while recording the entries in Journal or ledger.

What types of errors can trial balance identify?

1. Only one side of the entry is recorded in the General ledger.

Example: Sale of goods for cash $4000. Transaction is recorded in Cash a/c but missed to be recorded in sales a/c.

2. Once side of transaction is recorded with correct amount in GL but other side is recorded with wrong amount in other GL.

Example: Goods purchased with credit $5000. Purchase account is updated with an amount of $5000 but Account payable is updated with $4000.

3. Omission to post an account in trial balance.

Example: Rent paid $500. Cash a/c is taken to trial balance but Rent account is omitted and not taken to trial balance.

4. Wrong totaling of Ledger or sub Ledgers

Example: Account receivable account total is $2000. But it is wrongly totaled to $2500. In such case the Closing balance of Accounts receivable will wrongly increase by $500.

5. Posting on the wrong side.

Example: Salaries paid $500. This is recorded in the credit side of salaries account.

What types of error trial balance cannot identify?

1. Errors of principle: any error which violates the fundamental principles of accounting.

Example: Building purchased worth $50000. But this is recorded in the expenses account.

2. Errors of omission: any transaction which is not recorded in the Journal.

Example: Good purchased for $3000. It is not recorded in the Journal. Since both aspects of transactions are not recorded in the Journal and General ledger, Trial balance will tally.

3. Posting in a wrong account but in correct side.

Example: Rent paid of $2000 is recorded in Salaries account in debit side. In this case it is obviously wrong to record the rent paid in salaries account but trial balance will not be able to identify this because debit of salary account will match with the credit of cash account.

4. Error in the Journal book.

Example: *Salaries paid to employees worth $5000 is recorded as $500. In this case the General Leger account of salary will be debited with $500 and Cash account will be credited with$500. Trial balance will tally and the error could not be identified.*

5. Compensating errors: when one error compensates the other.

Example: Rent *paid $2000. But recorded as 1500. Rent account debited with $1500 but cash account credited with 2000. Excess credit balance is $500. There is an imbalance in accounts. Now, suppose another entry related to salaries paid worth $2000 is recorded as $2500 in salaries account. Salaries account is debited with $2500 but cash account is credited with 2000. Excess debit balance is $500. The excess credit balance from rent transaction will cancel out the excess debit balance of salaries transaction. The trial balance will tally.*

6. An entry is recorded in journal and Ledger more than one time

Example: Commissions paid $700. It is recorded two times in Commissions and Cash a/c. This error cannot be identified by trail balance.

CHAPTER 5 - ADJUSTING ENTRIES

Chapter Overview

1. Adjusting entries

2. Adjusted Trial balance

People often find adjusting entries complicated. I will make it simple for you and you will be able to understand them easily. Read each of adjustment, understand it and think about it and then move to other adjustment. At first reading these may appear confusing but once you fully understand them they will appear easy.

Section 1. Adjusting entries

What are adjusting entries?

1. At end of the period, mostly last date of your books close, you may have accounts that **do not reflect the correct balances as per accrual principle.**

2. You may have expenses incurred but that is not yet paid, incomes earned but not yet received, Depreciation not yet provided etc. These transactions needs to be recorded to adjust the ledger accounts.

3. Almost always, adjusting entries involve **one balance sheet account** and **one income statement account** (P/L account). The logic is one side of transaction will be expense or income and another side of transaction will be a receivable or payable.

4. Adjustments can be directly recorded by adjusting the accounts in P/L account or Balance sheet.

5. **Or** we can adjust the Ledger accounts first. **Prepare an adjusted trial balance.** Then from adjusted trial balance we can prepare the income statement and Balance sheet. This approach is preferable. At the end of this chapter I will show you how to prepare an adjusted trial balance.

Let us discuss some important adjusting entries.

1. Outstanding expenses:

These are the expenses which are ***accrued and due for payment*** but not yet paid

*For example, your company XYZ Ltd. has taken a building on rent from ABC Ltd. for its business. Rent **due** for the month of December 2017 is $500 but it is **not paid** as of 31/12/2017. Assume XYZ ltd. prepares its financial statements monthly.*

How to think?

*Point 1: Building is used in December. So Rent for the use of building is **accrued** or incurred in December. Since rent is payable at December end it is **due** also.*

Point 2: As per the accrual concept, expenses are recorded in the period in which they incur and not in the period in which they are paid.

Point 3: Since the company has not made the payment yet, it has to recognize the liability of Rent payable.

In the books of company XYZ – 31st December 2017

Date	Partiulars	Debit	Credit
31/12/2017	Rent a/c	500	
	Outstanding rent a/c		500

Profit and Loss account				Credit
	Debit			
Rent a/c	500			

Balance Sheet				
Equuity and liability			Assets	
Capital	XXX			
Liabililty				
Outstanding rent a/c	500			

What happens in next period?

1. Rent for December is not paid in January 2018.

Rent outstanding of $500 will be carried to February. The balance will be carried forward until it is paid

2. Rent for December is paid in January 2018

Method 1: Reverse the accrual booked in the previous month and recognize the rent paid.

a. Reversal of accrual.

This will nullify the effect of accrual booked in the previous month. However **it *will create a credit balance in the rent account.***

b. Recognize the payment for previous month's rent.

Rent account will be debited and cash account will be credited. The overall effect of the above entries will be accrued rent account of previous month will be zero and rent reported also becomes zero. This is correct as per accrual principle as we have already recognized this rent in December 2017.

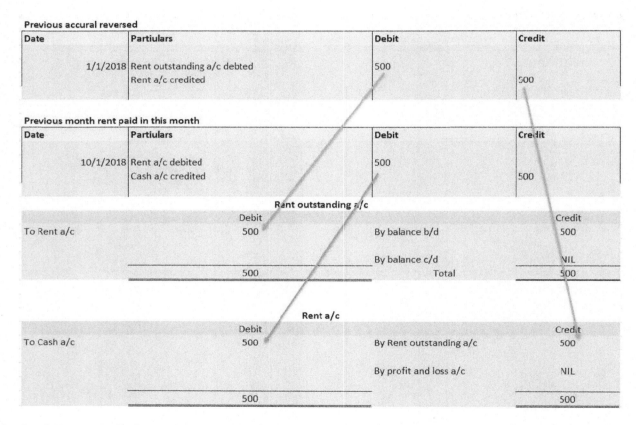

Previous accural reversed

Date	Partiulars	Debit	Credit
1/1/2018	Rent outstanding a/c debted	500	
	Rent a/c credited		500

Previous month rent paid in this month

Date	Partiulars	Debit	Credit
10/1/2018	Rent a/c debited	500	
	Cash a/c credited		500

Rent outstanding a/c

	Debit		Credit
To Rent a/c	500	By balance b/d	500
		By balance c/d	NIL
	500	Total	500

Rent a/c

	Debit		Credit
To Cash a/c	500	By Rent outstanding a/c	500
		By profit and loss a/c	NIL
	500		500

Method 2: Set off the accrual of previous month against the cash payment. This will make outstanding rent of previous month NIL.

Previous outstanding paid in cash

Date	Partiulars	Debit	Credit
10/1/2018	Rent outstanding a/c debited	500	
	Cash a/c credited		500

Rent outstanding a/c

	Debit		Credit
To Cash	500	By Balance b/d	500
To balance b/d	NIL		
	500	Total	500

Method 1 is preferable to method 2.

*Example: Rent of the building until December 2017 was $500. Rent payment that was outstanding in December is paid in January 2018. **Total cash paid for rent in January 1075**. There has been an increase in rent from January 2017.*

In case we follow method 2 and-

Forget to adjust the accrual: Rent recognized for January will be 1075. Which is wrong as it includes the rent amount of December also.

Total rent paid in January 2018

Date	Partiulars	Debit	Credit
10/1/2018	Rent a/c debited	1075	
	Cash a/c credited		1075

Want to recognize January amount correctly:

1. First we need to identify the January rent amount and record the same.

2. And need to adjust the accrued rent of previous month.

Total rent paid in January 2018

Date	Partiulars	Debit	Credit
10/1/2018	Rent a/c debited	575	
	Outstanding rent a/c debited	500	
	To Cash a/c		1075

However if we follow method 1:

No need to worry about the effect of previous month rent in this period.

1. Reversal of accrual nullifies the effect of previous month accrual and create a credit balance in rent account.

2. Total rent paid in cash is recorded in the debit side of rent account.

2. Rent account balance automatically reflects this month's balance.

Previous accural reversed

Date	Partiulars	Debit	Credit
1/1/2018	Rent outstanding a/c debted	500	
	Rent a/c credited		500

Total rent received in cash is $1075

Rent a/c

	Debit		Credit
To Cash a/c	1075	By Rent outstanding a/c	500
		By profit and loss a/c (Current month's rent)	575
	1075		1075

*Method 1 is particularly useful in the cases, where we don't know the actual amount we are going to pay for the expenses while finalizing the accounts. For example, electricity bill. We are going to create a **provision** on the basis of estimated amount, reverse the provision in the next month and book the actual amount.*

Note: if we follow this method **as a standard practice (means all the accruals booked in the previous month is reversed as a standard practice or automated within system),** we need to see whether the actual amount of previous month is paid in the current period or not. For example, if the December rent is still not paid in January and we have reversed the December accrual in January; what should be the process? **We need to create a new accrual for both December and January amounting $1075.**

Note: Both the methods are correct. It is up to you to decide which method to follow.

2. Outstanding Incomes:

These are the incomes which are *accrued and due* but not yet received.

For example, from the perspective company **ABC Ltd.**, which is in the business of letting out properties, rent due for the month of December 2017 is not received as of 31/12/2017.

How to think?

Point 1: Rent is to be received for building which is let out in December. So income from rental service is **earned** in December. Since it is receivable in December as per agreement it is **due** also.

Point 2: As per the accrual concept, incomes are recorded in the period in which they are earned and not in the period in which they are received in cash.

Point 3: Since the building owner has not received the income yet, he has to recognize it as a receivable (asset) - Accrued income.

In the books of ABC ltd. 31ˢᵗ December 2017

Date	Partiulars	Debit	Credit
31/12/2017	Accured rent a/c	500	
	Rent a/c		500

	Profit and Loss account		
	Debit		**Credit**
	Rent		500

Balance Sheet		
Equity and Liability	**Assets**	
Owner's equity	Non-current assets	
Current liabilities	Current assets	
	Accured rent	500.00

What happens in next period?

1. Rent for December 2017 is not received in January 2018

Carry forward the balance of Accrued rent until it is received.

2. Rent for December 2017 is received in January 2018

Method 1:

1. **Reverse the accrual booked in the previous month.**

This will nullify the effect of accrual booked in the previous month. However *it will create a debit balance in the rent income account.*

b. **Recognize the receipt for previous month's rent.**

Cash account will be debited and rent account will be credited. The overall effect of the above entries will be, accrued rent account of previous month will be zero and rent income reported also becomes zero.

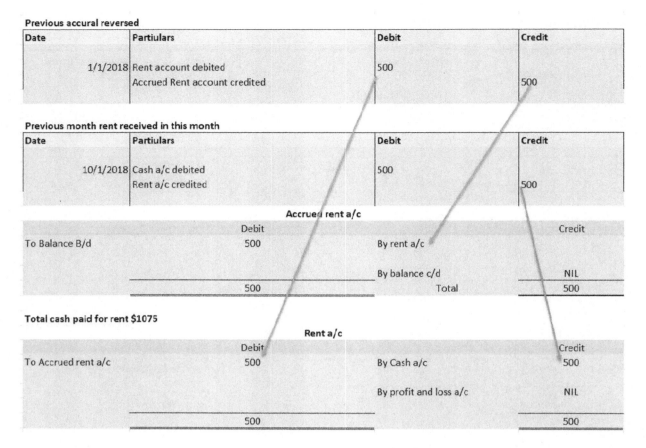

Previous accural reversed

Date	Partiulars	Debit	Credit
1/1/2018	Rent account debited	500	
	Accrued Rent account credited		500

Previous month rent received in this month

Date	Partiulars	Debit	Credit
10/1/2018	Cash a/c debited	500	
	Rent a/c credited		500

Accrued rent a/c

	Debit		Credit
To Balance B/d	500	By rent a/c	
		By balance c/d	NIL
	500	Total	500

Total cash paid for rent $1075

Rent a/c

	Debit		Credit
To Accrued rent a/c	500	By Cash a/c	500
		By profit and loss a/c	NIL
	500		500

Method 2: Set off the accrual of previous month against the cash payment. This will make Accrued rent account NIL.

Previous outstanding rent received in Cash

Date	Partiulars	Debit	Credit
10/1/2018	Cash a/c debited	500	
	Accrued rent a/c		500

Accrued Rent a/c

	Debit		Credit
To Balance b/d	500	By Cash	500
		By balance b/d	NIL
	500	Total	500

Method 1 is preferable to method 2.

Example: Rent of the building until December 2017 was $500. Rent income which was outstanding in December is received in January 2018. Total cash received for rent in January $1075. There has been an increase in rent from January 2017

In case we follow method 2 and-

Forget to adjust the accrual: Rent recognized for January will be 1075. Which is wrong as it includes the rent amount of December also.

Total rent recived in cash in January 2018

Date	Partiulars	Debit	Credit
10/1/2018	Cash a/c	1075	
	Rent a/c		1075

Want to recognize January amount correctly:

1. First we need to identify the January rent amount and record the same.

2. And need to adjust the accrued rent of previous month

Total rent recived in cash in January 2018

Date	Partiulars	Debit	Credit
10/1/2018	Cash a/c	1075	
	Rent a/c	.	500
	Accured rent a/c		575

However if we follow method 1:

No need to worry about the effect of previous month rent in this period.

1. Reversal of accrual nullifies the effect of previous month accrual and create a debit balance in rent account

2. Total rent received in January 2018 will be recorded in the credit side of the rent account.

3. Rent account balance automatically reflects current month's balance.

Previous accural reversed

Date	Partiulars	Debit	Credit
1/1/2018	Rent a/c debted	500	
	Accrued Rent a/c credited		500

Total rent received in cash is $1075

Rent a/c

	Debit		Credit
To Accrued rent a/c	500	By Cash a/c	1075
To profit and loss a/c (Rent of the month)	575		
	1075		1075

Note: if we follow this method **as a standard practice (means all the accruals booked in the previous month is reversed as a standard practice or automated within system)** , we need to see whether the actual amount of previous month is received in the current period or not. For example, if the December rent is still not received in January and we have reversed the December accrual in January; what should be the process? **We need to create a new accrual for both December and January amounting $1075.**

Note: Both the methods are correct. It is up to you to decide which method to follow.

3. Expenses accrued but not due

These are expenses which are *accrued but not yet due* for payment. It is easier for you to understand this if I explain it through an example.

XYZ ltd taken a bank loan $1000 in January 2018 at 1% monthly interest rate. The interest is paid quarterly. So the next payment of interest will be due for payment in March 2018.

How to record interest expenses in the January to March books?

How to think?

Point 1: As per the accrual concept, expenses are recorded in the period in which they are incurred and not in the period in which they are paid.

Point 2: Loan is taken in January and it is available for utilization. Although the interest is **not due yet**, interest expenses **needs to be accrued** for January.

Point 3. 'Interest accrued but not due' will be recognized as a liability.

In the books of XYZ ltd:

January 2018

Date	Partiulars	Debit	Credit
31/1/2018	Interest a/c To Interest accrued but not due	100	100

February 2018

Date	Partiulars	Debit	Credit
28/2/2018	Interest a/c To Interest accrued but not due	100	100

March 2018

Date	Partiulars	Debit	Credit
31/3/2018	Interest a/c To outstanding interest a/c	100	100

In this month the interest will be due for payment

1. March interest due $100

2. Interest is due for January and February also.

Date	Partiulars	Debit	Credit
31/3/2018	interest accrued but not due a/c outstanding interest a/c	200	200

Outstanding Interest

Debit			Credit	
		By interest (for March)		100
		By interest accrued but not due		200
To balance c/d	300			300
	300			300

Interest accrued but not due

Debit			Credit	
		By interest (Jan)		100
To interest accrued but not du	200	By interest (feb)		100
	200			200

Interest accrued but not due account becomes NIL as the amount for January and February become due. Total interest due is $300 which is the balance in Interest payable account/outstanding interest a/c.

If interest is not paid in March: Follow the same adjustments as discussed in Point 1: outstanding expenses.

4. Income accrued but not due

These are the income which are *accrued but not yet due*. Let us take the same example, but think from the angle of Banker

*XYZ ltd taken a loan in January from ABC Ltd. in January 2018 amounting $1000 at 1% monthly interest rate. The interest is paid quarterly. So the next payment of interest will be **due for payment in March** 2018.*

How to record interest incomes in the January to March books of Bank?

How to think?

Point 1: As per the accrual concept, incomes are recorded in the period in which they are earned and not in the period in which they are received.

Point 2: Loan is given in January and it is available as an asset from January. Although the interest is **not due to be received yet**, interest income **needs to be accrued** for January and February.

Point 3. 'Interest accrued but not due' will be recognized as an asset.

In the books of XYZ ltd

In January 2018

Date	Partiulars	Debit	Credit
31/1/2018	Interest accured but not due a/c To interest a/c	100	100

In February 2018

Date	Partiulars	Debit	Credit
28/2/2018	Interest accured but not due a/c To interest a/c	100	100

In March 2018

In this month the interest will be due for receipt

1. March interest due: $100

Date	Partiulars	Debit	Credit
31/3/2018	Accrued interest To interest a/c	100	100

2. Interest is due for January and February also.

Date	Partiulars	Debit	Credit
31/3/2018	Accrued interest	200	
	interest accrued but not due a/c		200

Accrued Interset

	Debit		Credit
To interest (for March)	100		
To interest accrued but not du	200		
		By balance c/d	300
	300		300

Interest accrued but not due

	Debit		Credit
To interest (Jan)	100	By Accrued interest	200
To interest (feb)	100		
	200		200

Interest accrued but not due account becomes NIL as the amount for January and February become due. Total interest due is $300 which is the balance in Interest receivable or Accrued interest account.

If interest is not received in March: Follow the same adjustments as discussed in Point 2: Accrued incomes

5. Prepaid expenses:

These are the expenses which are ***paid in advance but not yet incurred***.

Continuing the same example of Rent, let us assume XYZ ltd has paid three months advance rent in December 1 2017. Rent for December 2017 to February 2018 each month is $500.

How to think?

Point 1: Rent in paid in advance in the beginning of December for next three month. So the rental expenses will incur in December, January and February.

Point 2: As per the accrual concept, expenses are recorded in the period in which they are incurred and not in the period in which they are paid.

Point 3. Follow either the **asset method** or **expense method** for recognizing prepaid rent.

There are ***two methods*** for initial recording of prepaid expenses.

Books of XYZ ltd:

Asset Method: In this method the advance rent is recorded **as asset** and then transferred to rent expense account once it is incurred or used up.

December 1

Date	Partiulars	Debit	Credit
1/12/2017	Prpaid Rent a/c	1500	
	To Cash a/c		1500

What happens in the end of December, January and February?

1. at the end of December: Rent is incurred for December as building is used in this period. So rent expenses for this period needs to be recognized prepaid rent is reduced by 500 as it is utilized in this period. Prepaid rent balance = 1500 – 500 =1000

Date	Partiulars	Debit	Credit
31/12/2017	Rent expenses a/c	500	
	To prepaid Rent		500

2. at the end of January: Rent is incurred for January as building is used in this period. So rent expenses for this period needs to be recognized Prepaid rent is reduced by 500 as it is utilized for January. Prepaid rent balance = 1000 – 500 =500

Date	Partiulars	Debit	Credit
31/1/2018	Rent expenses a/c	500	
	To prepaid rent		500

3. at the end of February: Rent is incurred for February as building is used in this period. So rent expenses for this period needs to be recognized

Prepaid rent is reduced by 500 as it is utilized in this period. Prepaid rent balance = 500 – 500 = 0

Date	Partiulars	Debit	Credit
28/2/2018	Rent expense a/c	500	
	Prepaid rent a/c		500

Prepaid rent a/c

	Debit		Credit
To cash	1500	By rent (dec)	500
		By rent(Jan)	500
		By rent (feb)	500
		By Balance c/d	NIL
	1500		1500

Note: Rent expense of each months should be transferred to income statement and closed.

Expense Method: In this method the total rent paid is recorded as an expense in the period of payment. At the end of the month it is adjusted for rent which is not incurred yet.

THINK LIKE AN ACCOUNTANT

December 1

Date	Partiulars	Debit	Credit
1/12/2017	Rent expenses a/c Cash	1500	1500

What happens in the end of December, January and February?

1. at the end of December: Rent is incurred for December as building is used in this period. But the rent for January and February is still not incurred. So the rent pertaining to January and February should be **deferred** and recognized as asset.

Date	Partiulars	Debit	Credit
31/12/2017	Prepaid rent a/c To Rent a/c	1000	1000

2. at the end of January: Rent is incurred for February as building is used in this period. So rent expenses for this period needs to be recognized and prepaid rent needs to be reduced.

Date	Partiulars	Debit	Credit
31/1/2018	Rent a/c To Prepaid rent a/c	500	500

Prepaid rent is reduced by 500 as it is utilized for February. Prepaid rent balance = 1000 – 500 =500

3. at the end of February: Rent is incurred for March as building is used in this period. So rent expenses for this period needs to be recognized.

Date	Partiulars	Debit	Credit
28/2/2018	Rent a/c To Prepaid rent a/c	500	500

Prepaid rent is reduced by 500 as it is utilized in this period. Prepaid rent balance = 500 – 500 = 0

Prepaid rent account

	Debit		Credit
To rent a/c (dec. end)	1000		
		By rent a/c (jan)	500
		By rent a/c (feb)	500
		By Balance c/d	NIL
	200		200

69

Note: Rent expense of each months should be transferred to income statement and closed.

6. Income received in Advance

These are the incomes which are *received in advance but not yet earned*.

Continuing the same example of Rent, let us assume XYZ ltd has received three months advance rent in December 1 2017. Rent for December to February each month is $500.

How to think?

Point 1: Rent received in advance in the beginning of December for next three month. So the rental income will be earned in December, January and February.

Point 2: As per the accrual concept, incomes are recorded in the period in which they are earned and not in the period in which they are received.

Point 3. Follow either the *Liability method* or *income method* for recognizing rent received in advance.

There are **two methods** for initial recording of income received in advance.

Books of XYZ ltd:

Liability Method: In this method the advance rent is **recorded as liability** (since it is not earned yet) and then transferred to rent income account once it is earned.

1. December 1

Date	Partiulars	Debit	Credit
1/12/2017	Cash a/c	1500	
	To Rental Income received in advance		1500

What happens in the end of December, January and February?

1. at the end of December: Rent is earned for December as building is let out in this period. So rent income for this period needs to be recognized and liability of rental income received in advance should be reduced.

Date	Partiulars	Debit	Credit
31/12/2017	Rental income received in advance	500	
	To Rent a/c		500

Advance rent received liability is reduced by 500 as it is utilized in this period. Advance rent balance = 1500 – 500 =1000

2. at the end of January: Rent is earned for January as building is let out in this period. So rent income for this period needs to be recognized.

Date	Partiulars	Debit	Credit
31/1/2018	Rental income received in Advance a/c To Rent a/c	500	500

Advance rent received liability is reduced by 500 as it is utilized in this period. Advance rent balance = 1000 – 500 =500

3. at the end of February: Rent is earned for February as building is let out in this period. So rent income for this period needs to be recognized.

Date	Partiulars	Debit	Credit
28/2/2018	Rental income received in Advance a/c To Rent a/c	500	500

Advance rent received liability is reduced by 500 as it is utilized in this period. Advance rent balance = 500 – 500 =0.

Rental income recived in advance			
	Debit		Credit
To Rent (dec.)	500	By Cash	1500
To rent a/c (jan)	500		
To Rent (feb.)	500		
To Balance c/d	**NIL**		
	1500		1500

Note: Rent income of each months should be transferred to income statement and closed.

Income Method: In this method the total rent received is ***recorded as an income*** in the period of receipt. At the end of the month it is adjusted for rent which is not earned yet.

On December 1

Date	Partiulars	Debit	Credit
1/12/2017	Cash a/c To Rental income	1500	1500

What happens in the end of December, January and February?

1. at the end of December: Rent is earned for December as building is let out this period. But the rent for January and February is still not earned. So the rent pertaining to January and February should be **deferred** and recognized as liability.

Date	Partiulars	Debit	Credit
31/12/2017	Rental income a/c	1000	
	To Rental income received in advance		1000

2. at the end of January: Rent is earned for January as building is let out in this period. So rent income for this period needs to be recognized.

Date	Partiulars	Debit	Credit
31/1/2018	Rental income receive in advance a/c	500	
	To Rent a/c		500

Advance rent received liability is reduced by 500 as it is utilized in this period. Advance rent balance = 1000 – 500 =500

3. at the end of February: Rent is earned for February as building is let out in this period. So rent income for this period needs to be recognized.

Date	Partiulars	Debit	Credit
28/2/2018	Rental income received in advance	500	
	To rental income		500

Advance rent received liability is reduced by 500 as it is utilized in this period. Advance rent balance = 500 – 500 =0

Rental income recived in advance			
Debit		Credit	
		By Rent income	1000
To rent income a/c (jan)	500		
To Rent income (feb.)	500		
To Balance c/d	**NIL**		
	1500		1000

Note: Rent expense of each months should be transferred to income statement and closed.

7. Other Adjustments

It is possible to have several other adjustments but below are the three important adjustments which we will discuss as parts of three different chapters

1. Depreciation: see Appendix 2 "Depreciation" for details calculation and treatment for depreciation

2. Closing stock: see Appendix 3 'Inventory and cost of goods sold'

 3. Bad debt, allowance for doubtful debt, provision for discount on debtors: see Appendix 4 'Accounts receivable Adjustments'

Section 2. Adjusted Trial Balance

The trial balance which is *prepared after posting the Adjusting Journal entries to the ledger accounts* is called Adjusted Trial balance.

Let's understand this through an example.

Below is an **unadjusted** Trial Balance **as on 31/12/2017**

Particulars (Ledger a/c ending balances)	Debit ($)	Credit ($)
Captial		20,000.00
Long term loans		9,000.00
Accounts payable		5,000.00
Short term loans		7,000.00
Building	10,000.00	
Machinary	6,000.00	
Investments	1,000.00	
Land	4,000.00	
Furniture	2,000.00	
Accounts receivable	4,000.00	
Cash	8,000.00	
Bank	6,000.00	
Purchases	3,000.00	
Salaries	1,000.00	
Rent	800.00	
Advertisiing expenses	5,000.00	
Gain from sale of Fixed assets		4,500.00
Interest income		300.00
Sales		5,000.00
Total	50,800.00	50,800.00

Adjustments

1. Rent payable for the month of December is $1500. $700 is yet to be paid.

2. Advertisement expenses paid in advance for five months from December 2017 to April 2018.

3. Interest accrued for the month of December 2017 $500. $200 is yet to be received.

How to prepare the adjusted trial balance?

Step 1. Record the adjusting Journal entries

Step 2. Post the adjusting Journal entries to ledger accounts and find the closing balance.
(For the income and expenses accounts closing balance is the balance that will be transferred to P/L a/c)

Step 3. Prepare adjusted trial balance from the adjusted ledger accounts.

Now let's proceed with our example:

Step 1 and 2. Record the adjusting Journal entries and posting to ledger.

1. Rent payable for the month of November is $1500. $700 is yet to be paid.

Date	Partiulars	Debit	Credit
31/12/2017	Rent a/c Rent Outstanding a/c	700	700

Rent a/c

	Debit		Credit
To Cash	800		
To Rent Outstanding a/c	700		
	1500		1500

Rent Outstanding a/c

	Debit		Credit
		By Rent	700
To balance c/d	700		
	700		700

2. Advertisement expenses paid in advance for five months from November 2017 to March 2018. Monthly expenses is $1000.

Date	Partiulars	Debit	Credit
31/12/2017	Prepaid Advertisng expense a/c Advertising expenses a/c	4000	4000

Advertising expenses a/c

Debit		Credit	
To Cash	5000		
		By Prepaid advertising exp. a/c	4000
		By profit and loss a/c	1000
	5000		5000

Prepaid advertising expenses a/c

Debit		Credit	
To Advertising exp. a/c	4000		
		By Balance c/d	4000
	4000		4000

3. Interest accrued for the month of November 2017 $500. $200 is yet to be received.

Date	Partiulars	Debit	Credit
31/12/2017	Accrued interest a/c interest a/c	200	200

Interest a/c

Debit		Credit	
		By Cash	300
		By Accued interest	200
By Profit and loss a/c	500		
	500		500

Accrued interest a/c

Debit		Credit	
To interest a/c	200		
		By Balance c/d	200
	4000		4000

Step 3. Prepare adjusted trial balance from the adjusted ledger accounts.

Adjusted trial balance as on 31/12/2017

Particulars (Ledger a/c ending balances)				Debit ($)	Credit ($)
Captial					20,000.00
Long term loans					9,000.00
Accounts payable					5,000.00
Short term loans					7,000.00
Rent Outstanding a/c					**700.00**
Building				10,000.00	
Machinary				6,000.00	
Investments				1,000.00	
Land				4,000.00	
Furnitures				2,000.00	
Accounts receivable				4,000.00	
Cash				8,000.00	
Bank				6,000.00	
Prepaid Adverstining a/c				**4,000.00**	
Accrued interset a/c				200.00	
Purchases				3,000.00	
Salaries				1,000.00	
Rent				1,500.00	
Advertisiing expenses				**1,000.00**	
Gain from sale of Fixed assets					4,500.00
Interest income					500.00
Sales					5,000.00
Total				51,700.00	51,700.00

Note:

1. You can observe one PL account and one balance sheet account is getting affected.

2. You can directly make these adjustments in profit and loss a/c and Balance sheet without preparing the adjusted trial balance. It is recommended to prepare the adjusted trial balance because you can check the accuracy of your postings.

CHAPTER 6 - INCOME STATEMENT

Chapter overview:

Section 1: Income statement

Section 2: Closing entries

Section 3: Statement of retained earnings

Section 1: Income statement

This is also called profit and loss account. It records Revenue, Income, Expenses, losses and gains. It includes all the temporary accounts. This statement helps to identify the performance of the business in terms of profit and loss.

Structure of Income statement: The structure of income statement can be either a statement type or an account type. In some countries it is mandatory to follow a specific structure prescribed by the Accounting standards applicable to that country. For Easy understanding I will provide here a simple structures of income statement or profit and loss a/c.

TYPE-I

Income statement for the month/year ended 31-12-2017	Amount ($)	Amount ($)
Revenue		
Less: Sales return	XXX	
Less: Discount	XXX	
Net Revenue	XXX	XXX
Less: Cost of Goods sold		XXX
Gross profit		XXX
Administative expences	XXX	XXX
Selling and disribution expenses	XXX	
Total operating expenses	XXX	(XXX)
Operating profit or Loss (GP- OE)		XXX
Interest incomes		
Gain on sale of fixed assets		
Interest expenses		
Loss from sale of fixed assets		
Good destroyed due to fire		
Penalties		
Loss from Law suit		
Total Non operating incomes and expenses	XXX	(XXX)
Net profit or Loss		XXX

TYPE II

Income statement for the month/year ended 31-12-2017					
		Debit ($)			Credit ($)
Opening stock			Revenues	XXX	
Purchases	XXX		Less: Sales Return	(XXX)	
Less: Purchase return	(XXX)		Less: Discount	(XXX)	
Less: purchse discount	(XXX)		Net Revenue		XXX
Net Purchases		XXX			
Carriege inward		XXX			
Direct expenses		XXX	Closing stock		XXX
Gross profit		XXX	Gross loss		
		XXX			XXX
			Gross Profit		XXX
Operating expenses		XXX	Interest incomes		XXX
Administative expences		XXX	Gain on sale of fixed assets		XXX
Selling and disribution expenses		XXX			
Other expenses					
Non operating expenses					
Interest expenses		XXX			
Loss from sale of fixed assets		XXX			
Good destroyed due to fire		XXX			
Penalties		XXX			
Loss from Law suit		XXX			
Net Profit			**Net Loss**		XXX
		XXX			XXX

NOTE:

1. **Revenue**: it is the income generated from selling goods or provision of services.

2. **Cost of Goods sold:** opening stock of inventory + purchases + direct expenses – Closing stock **(More discussion on cost of goods sold is given in Appendix 3- Inventory and cost of goods sold)**

3. **Gross profit:** Net sales less Cost of Goods sold.

4. **Operating expenses:** These are the expenses associated with the main operating activities of business. For example: CGS, Administrative expenses, Selling and distribution expenses.

5. **Operating incomes** are generated from the main activities of business. For example: Selling of goods or provision of services

5. **Direct expenses:** These are expenses directly associated with production of goods or services and forms part of costs of goods sold.

6. The first part of **TYPE II format of Income** statement up to gross profit and loss is sometimes called **Trading account.** This account is normally maintained under 'periodic inventory system' (Detailed explanation is given in **Appendix 3- Inventory and cost of goods sold)**

7. **Non-operating expenses:** these are expenses which are not related to the main activities of business. For example: interest expense, loss on sale of fixed assets.

8. **Non-operating incomes:** these are incomes which are not related to the main activities of business. For example: interest income, Gain on sale of fixed assets.

9. **Administrative expenses:** These are the expenses made for the day today management of business. This includes rent, salaries, depreciation on office building, depreciation on furniture and fixtures, audit fees, insurance, other employee benefits etc.

10. **Selling and distribution expenses:** These expense are operating expenses associated with sales, marketing and distribution of goods and services. For example: Sales commission, salary of sales person, Advertisement expenses etc.

11. **Net profit:** Gross profit less all other expenses. If it is negative, it is called Net Loss.

Section 2: Closing entries

Closing entries are transferring entries **used to transfer the balances in income and expenses accounts to the Income statement** or profit and loss account. Some people use another account called Income summary account to close the incomes and expenses. In this way the balances of all the income, gains, losses and expenses account becomes NIL.

 Example: Below are the GL account balances of different income and expenses accounts at the end of the year. Prepare closing entry for transferring these balances to income statement.

1. Cash sales a/c $5000

2. Credit sales a/c $2000

3. Purchase of goods a/c $4500

4. Closing stock a/c $1000

5. Rent paid a/c $500

6. Salaries paid $1000

7. Commissions paid $400

8. Interest income $300

Closing entry:

1. Transferring the Credit balance accounts.

Date	Partiulars	Debit	Credit
31/12/2018	Cash sales a/c	5000	
	Credit sales a/c	2000	
	interest income a/c	300	
	Closing stock a/c	1000	
	To profit and loss a/c		8300

2. Transferring the Debit balance accounts.

Date	Partiulars	Debit	Credit
31/12/2018	Profit and loss a/c	6400	
	To purchases		4500
	To rent a/c		500
	To Salaries a/c		1000
	To commission a/c		400

Profit and loss account after closing entries are booked.

Income statement for the month/year ended 31-12-2017					
		Debit ($)			**Credit ($)**
Opening stock			Cash sales	5000	
			Credit Sales	2000	
Purchases	4500		Less: Sales Return	NIL	
Less: Purchase return	NIL		Less: Discount	NIL	
Less: purchse discount	NIL		Net Revenue		7000
Net Purchases		4500			
			Closing stock		1000
Gross profit		3500	Gross loss		
		8000			8000
			Gross Profit		3500
Operating expenses			Interest incomes		300
Rent		500			
Salaries		1000			
Commission		400			
Non operating expenses		NIL			
Net Profit		1900			
		3800			3800

Section 3: Statement of Retained earnings

You are aware that any net profit and net loss made by the business at the end of the accounting period belongs to owners or shareholders of business. **When the company distributes such profits, it is called dividends.** The undistributed profit is retained in an account called retained earnings account. The net profit and loss made during the year is transferred to this account first. Then if company decides to pay dividends, amount is paid from this account. This account act as a bridge between income statement and balance sheet.

Let's take an example and draw statement of retained earnings.

A ltd. has an opening balance of retained earnings $3000

Company has made profit during the year 2017 amounting $1000

It decided to pay dividends of $300

Prepare statement of Retained earnings and show where is shown in the balance sheet.

Statement of Retained earnings as on 31-12-2017	Amount ($)
Opening balance as on 1-1-2017	3,000.00
Profit made during 2017	1,000.00
Less: Dividends paid	(300.00)
Closing balance	3,700.00

Balance Sheet			
Equuity and liability		Assets	
Capital	XXX	Non current assets	XXX
Retained earnings	3700		
		Current Assets	
Liabiliity		Accrued rent	XXX
	XXX		XXX

CHAPTER 7 - BALANCE SHEET

Balance sheet **is a detailed representation of accounting equation**. It contains assets, liabilities and owner's equity. It is prepared at the end of accounting period to evaluate the financial position of business.

Below is a simple format of Balance sheet.

Balance Sheet			
Equity and liability		**Assets**	
Owner's equity Capital Retained earnings Other reserves **Non-current liabilities** Long term loans **Current liabilities** Accounts payable Bank overdraft Tax payable Outstanding expenses Income received in advance Expenses accrued but not due		**Non-current assets** Fixed assets (property, plants and equipment) Long term investments Intangible assets (goodwill, patents) **Current assets** Cash and cash equivalents Inventories Accounts receivable Short term investment Prepaid expenses Accrued incomes Expenses accrued but not due	

Let's take an example: Below is the **adjusted trial balance** of ABC ltd. Prepare the income statement and Balance sheet.

Particulars (Ledger a/c ending balances)	Debit ($)	Credit ($)
Captial		20,000.00
Long term loans		9,000.00
Accounts payable		5,000.00
Short term loans		7,000.00
Rent Outstanding a/c		700.00
Building	10,000.00	
Machinary	6,000.00	
Investments	1,000.00	
Land	4,000.00	
Furniture	2,000.00	
Accounts receivable	4,000.00	
Cash	8,000.00	
Bank	6,000.00	
Prepaid Adverstining a/c	4,000.00	
Accrued interset a/c	200.00	
Purchases	3,000.00	
Salaries	1,000.00	
Rent	1,500.00	
Advertisiing expenses	1,000.00	
Gain from sale of Fixed assets		4,500.00
Interest income		500.00
Sales		5,000.00
Total	51,700.00	51,700.00

Income statement: All the incomes and expenses accounts are transferred to the income statement by closing entry.

Income statement for the month/year ended 31-12-2017			
	Debit ($)		Credit ($)
Opening stock	NIL	Sales	5000
Purchases	3000		
		Closing stock	NIL
Gross profit	**2000**	Gross loss	
	5000		5000
		Gross Profit	**2000**
Operating expenses		Interest incomes	500
Rent	1500		
Salaries	1000	Gain from sale of fixed assets	4500
Advertisement expenses	1000		
Non operating expenses	NIL		
Net Profit	3500		
	7000		7000

Income statement for the year ended 31-12-2017

Statement of Retained earnings as on 31-12-2017			Amount ($)
Opening balance as on 1-1-2017			NIL
Profit made during 2017			3,500.00
Less: Dividends paid			NIL
Closing balance			3,500.00

Statement of Retained earnings as on 31-12-2017

Balance sheet as on 31-12-2017

Balance Sheet				
Equuity and liability		**Assets**		
Owner's equity		Non-current assets		
Capital	20000			
Retained earnings	3500	Building		10,000.00
Other reserves		Machinary		6,000.00
		Investments		1,000.00
Non-current liabilities		Land		4,000.00
Long term loans	9000	Furniture		2,000.00
Current liabilities		**Current assets**		
Accounts payable	5000	Accounts receivable		4,000.00
Short term loans	7000	Cash		8,000.00
Bank overdraft		Bank		6,000.00
Tax payable		Prepaid Advertisement		4,000.00
Rent outstanding	700	Accrued interest		200.00
Income received in advance		Expenses accrued but not due		
Expenses accrued but not due				
	45200			45,200.00

Note: Balance sheet shows us the financial position of the business at any point of time. The information contained in the Balance sheet is helpful in ascertaining the financial health of the business. There are many methods through which we can interpret the figures in the balance sheet. But that is the subject of another book.

Appendix 1 - Principles of Accounting World Continued

1. Principles related to Assets and liabilities

<u>Going concern:</u>

As per this principle, accountants assume that business will continue its operations in a foreseeable future. It is not going to liquidate (close down) in near future.

This principle is the basis for classifying the assets into current and non-current, deferring (postponing the recognition) expenses to future period, providing depreciation for assets. This concept is also the foundation of historical cost concept.

Example: You have taken a loan which will be paid over next 10 years. You will recognize this loan as a long term liability. You are assuming that business will continue its operations for next 10 years.

Example: Insurance premium paid in advance for 3 years. You will record this expense as an asset called prepaid insurance.

Example: A ltd. brought a building. The building has an estimated life of 5 years. Depreciation is calculated on this basis of estimated life. And the estimated life of an asset assumes that going concern assumption is valid.

Example: You brought a building at $10000 before one year. In the financial statements of your business the building will appear with a cost of $10000 although its market value may be different. If the going concern assumption is not valid, the building will be reported in its realizable value or market value.

<u>Historical cost principle.</u>

Assets and liabilities are recorded at the cost they are acquired. They should not be recorded at their realizable value or market value. The exception to this principle is where going concern assumption is not valid.

Example: You acquired a land at $12000 in 2015. The present market value of land is $15000. At which cost you should record the land in your business books?

As per the cost principle, the cost of land to be recorded in the books is $12000.

Note: Accounting standards of various countries and international financial reporting standards permit the use of revaluation model. As per this model the asset are revalued to the current market value.

2. Principles related to Incomes and expenses: Refer to chapter 3

3. Principles related to Owner's equity.

Business entity principle

As per this principle, accountants should assume the business as a separate entity from its owner. This is done in order to prevent the owners' personal transactions getting mixed with the transactions of business.

Example: A separate account for owner is maintained in business called owner's equity or capital account, where the capital contribution by owner is recorded. Any withdrawals by owner for his personal transactions reduces the owners' equity.

4. Principles related to overall preparation and presentation of financial statements.

Monetary unit principle

Business transactions and events are expressed in terms of money. Anything which is not quantifiable in terms of money is not recorded. For example, employee skills are not quantifiable and cannot be recorded. This principle ignore the effect of inflation on money.

Example: you have purchased 1000 units of inventories at $5000. In the general ledger account for purchases, only $5000 will be recorded. The information of 1000 units will not appear in the general ledger.

*Example: 10 acres of land are purchased for $1000 per acre in 1990. Land will be recorded at 10 * $1000 = $10000 in the financial statements even after 30 years. Present value of land may be $50000 due to inflation, but this principle ignores the value of inflation.*

Periodicity:

This principle divides the life of a business in shorter time periods. Normally it is one year. At the end of such period financial statements are prepared to ascertain the profit or loss made by the company and its financial position.

Consistency

The principles and methods of accounting should be applied consistently over a period of time. Financial statements of two periods cannot be compared if the accounting principles applied for the periods are not consistent. Hence *unless the change in policies results in a better presentation of financial statements or to comply with the accounting standards,* accountants should not change the accounting policies and principles. Any such change should be properly documented and the effect of such change should be assessed and reflected in the financial statements.

Materiality

As per this principle, accountants may ignore the guidelines of other principles if the amount is very small or immaterial. It is not defined what is material and immaterial, so this is a matter of accountant's professional judgement. An accountant should see, whether the amount is significant enough to affect the decision of users of financial statement. If yes, then it is material and if no, then it is immaterial.

3. Other relevant concepts

Temporary vs permanent accounts

Temporary accounts: These accounts accumulates the transactions for one year. At the end of the year these accounts these are closed to permanent accounts *through income statement*.

- Expenses accounts

- Revenue accounts

- Gain or loss accounts (example: profit or loss on sale of fixed assets)

Permanent accounts: these account which are maintained over more than one accounting period.

- Asset accounts

- Liability accounts

- Owner's equity account

- Retained earnings account

Note: Temporary accounts are incomes, expenses, revenue and gains are transferred to the income statement at the end of the accounting **period by passing closing entries.** The net result of income statement is then transferred to Retained earning account. Retaining earning account is a part of owner's equity account.

Appendix 2 - Depreciation

Fixed assets (tangible) are subject to depreciation.

Deprecation: fixed asset like building, machinery, plants are acquired to be used for more than one accounting period. The benefit from these assets is obtained over their life time. We need to spread the cost of acquiring these assets over their life time in a systematic way. ***This is in line with the matching concept.*** As the business start using the asset, in each accounting period the cost of the asset is reduced and charged as an expense to income statement. **This expense is called depreciation.**

Some of the terms you should be acquainted with in order to compute deprecation.

Depreciable cost: This is the acquisition cost of asset less salvage value (also called residual value)

Asset life : It is the estimated period over which the asset will be used.

Residual value: The business might expect to recover some amount by selling the asset at the end of its estimated life. It is called residual or salvage value.

Accumulated depreciation: it is a **contra asset account** in which we accumulate the depreciation expenses until the end of asset life or the sale of asset. It is shown in the balance sheet as a deduction from Asset account.

There are different ways to measure depreciation. We will discuss two important methods one by one.

Straight line method

This method is very simple. Under this method the depreciable cost is spread evenly over the life of the asset.

Example: ABC ltd. acquired a building at the cost of $10000 on 1-1-2017. It estimates the useful life of the building is 10 years. At the end of the asset life, ABC Ltd expects to realize $2000 from the sale of the building.

Depreciable value of the asset = Acquisition cost – Residual value = $10000 - $2000 = $8000.

Depreciation per year = Depreciable amount / asset life.

= $8000/10= $800 per year

*If ABC Ltd. is preparing yearly financial statement, at the end of each year for ten years it will pass the below journal entry. **Since depreciation is booked at the end of the period, it is booked as an adjusting entry.** I will show you the accounting flow for this method from journal to Balance* sheet. The flow of accounting will be same for other methods; only the amount calculated will be different.

Date	Partiulars	Debit	Credit
31/12/2017	Depreciation a/c To Accumulated depreciation a/c	800	800
31/12/2017	Profit and loss a/c To Depreciation a/c	800	800

Depreciation a/c

	Debit		Credit
To Accumulated depreciation a/c	800	By Profit and loss a,	800
	800		800

Accumulated depreciation a/c

		By Depreciation a/c	800
To balance c/d	800		
	800		800

Income statement for the year ended 31-12-2017			
	Debit ($)		Credit ($)
Opening stock		Sales	
Purchases			
		Closing stock	
Gross profit		Gross loss	
		Gross Profit	
Operating expenses			
Depreciation	800		
Non operating expenses			
Net Profit			

Balance Sheet as on 31-12-2017			
Equity and liability		Assets	
Owner's equity		Non-current assets	
		Building	10000
		Less: Accumulated Depreciation	800
		Net book Value	9,200.00
Current liabilities		Current assets	

Note: Same accounting process will be carried out at each year end for 10 years.

Written down value method

Under this method a fixed percentage is applied to the written down value of the asset to determine the depreciation.

Here, written down value (WDV) means Net book value at the beginning of the year. Net book value is acquisition value less accumulated depreciation up to that period.

Example: ABC ltd. acquired a building at the cost of $10000 on 1-1-2017. It estimates the useful life of the building is 10 years. It follows WDV method of depreciation and rate of depreciation is 10% per annum.

Depreciation amount: Net book value at the beginning of the year * 10%

Year	Net book Value at the beginning on the year	Depreciation for the year	Net book Value at the End on the year
2017	10,000	1000	9000
2018	9,000	900	8100
2019	8,100	810	7290
2020	7,290	729	6561
2021	6,561	656	5905
2022	5,905	590	5314
2023	5,314	531	4783
2024	4,783	478	4305
2025	4,305	430	3874
2026	3,874	387	3487

NOTE: under this method the book value of asset can never be zero at the end of the useful life.

How to determine the rate of deprecation?

Rate of depreciation under WDV method is ascertained by below formula:

$$\text{Depreciation Rate} = 100 \left(1 - n\sqrt{\frac{S}{C}} \right) \quad \text{where } n = \text{number of years}$$

$$S = \text{Salvage value}$$

$$C = \text{Cost of asset}$$

For example, a Machinery costs $ 8,000 with an estimated salvage value of $ 1,000. It has 3 years of useful life. The rate of depreciation will be calculated thus:

$$\text{Rate of Depreciation} = 100\left(1 - 3\sqrt{\frac{1000}{8000}}\right)$$

$$= 50\%$$

Treatment of Accumulated depreciation in case of sale of assets

Accumulated depreciation account is set off against the acquisition value of asset account as it is no longer needs to be maintained.

Example: ABC ltd had acquired an asset in 2012 with $12000. On 31/12/2017, it has sold the asset at $4000. Accumulated depreciation account as of 31/12/2017 has a balance of $6000.

Net book value of asset as on 31/12/2017 = Acquisition value (-) Accumulated depreciation = 12000 – 6000 = 6000.

Loss of asset sale = Amount received from sale (-) Net book value of asset

= 4000 – 6000 = 2000

Journal

Date	Partiulars	Debit	Credit
31/12/2017	Accoumulated depreciaion a/c Cash a/c Loss on sale of asset account To Asset a/c	6000 4000 2000	 12000

Appendix 3 - Inventory and Cost of Goods Sold

Section 1: Concepts

Section 2. Inventory systems

Section 3. Assignment of cost to inventory

Section 1. Underlying concepts

Inventories: Inventories are goods that are held for the purpose of sale. Wholesalers and retailers have finished goods as inventory whereas manufacturers can have inventories at different stages of production such as row materials, work in progress and finished goods. Inventories are shown as current assets in the balance sheet.

Accounting for inventories are driven by three accounting principles.

Cost principle: Inventories should be recorded at the cost in which they are acquired. Any subsequent change in the price of inventory in the market will not be considered.

Conservatism: If the inventories cannot be sold at the cost in which they are acquired, accountant needs to follow the conservative approach *and record the value at their net realizable value which is less than cost.*

Matching: Cost of inventories sold (CGS) need to be recorded when the corresponding revenue from sales of these inventories are recorded.

There are two components of inventory accounting

1. To identify the cost of goods sold and unsold inventory (closing stock)

2. To see whether unsold or closing inventory is realizable

Cost of Goods sold

This is the **cost** of the goods that has been sold to the customers. It is matched with the revenue to ascertain the gross profit.

CGS = (opening stock + purchases during the year) – closing stock

CGS = Total inventory available for sale – closing stock

Opening stock: Inventory at the beginning of the period.

Closing stock: unsold inventory at the end of period.

Purchases: Inventories purchased during the year.

Section 2. Inventory systems

There are two types inventory management system to keep track of inventory. Accounting of inventory depends on the inventory system company follows.

Perpetual inventory system

In this system inventories are **continuously updated** for

1. Inventories purchased

2. Inventories sold

3. Inventories returned to vendors

4. Inventories returned from customers

5. Direct expenses incurred on inventories

3. Inventories used in production

4. Inventories scrapped

5. Inventories transferred from one location to the other

It is preferred method of recording inventory movements because it has updated information at any point of time.

Accounting features

1. Inventory account is maintained as a current asset. All costs related to inventory and debited to this account. All decrease in cost is credited.

2. Costs of goods sold (CGS) is maintained to track cost of the goods reduced from inventory and sold to customers.

Common Journal entries for perpetual inventory system

Example:

1. Jan 1. Purchase goods on credit $2000.

2. Jan 5. Shipping expenses paid to receive goods $ 100

3. Jan 10. Sold goods for credit $1500. Cost of these goods were $1200.

4. Jan 10. Shipping expenses paid for delivery of Goods $50.

5. Jan 12. Return of goods purchased $500.

6. Jan 15. Paid to creditors $1300 (discount received $200).

7. Jan 20. Goods returned from customers priced at $500. Cost of these goods are 300.

8. Jan 25. Received payment from debtors in full settlement $900 (discount given $100)

Note: Full settlement means amount due is settled in full and there is no remaining balance to be paid or received.

Date	Partiulars		Debit	Credit
1/1/2017	**Purchases of Goods on credit.** *Inventory a/c* To Accounts payable		2000	2000
5/1/2017	**Shipping expenses paid to receive goods** *Inventory a/c* debited To Cash		100	100
10/1/2017	**Sold goods for credit $1500. Cost of these goods are $1200** *Cost of goods sold a/c* *Inventory a/c* *(recording of cost)* Accounts receivable a/c Sales *(Recording of revenue)*		1200 1500	1200 1500
10/1/2017	**Shipping expenses paid for delivery of goods** *Delivery expenses a/c* Cash a/c		50	50
12/1/2017	**Return of goods purchased $500** Accounts payable a/c *Inventory a/c*		500	500
15/1/2017	**Paid to creditors $1300 in full settlement** Accounts payable a/c To Cash *To inventory a/c*		1500	1300 200
20/1/2017	**Goods retutned from customers priced $500. Cost of these goods are $300** *Inventory a/c* Cost of goods sold a/c *(recording of expenses decrease)* Sales return a/c Accounts receivable a/c *(Recording of revenue decresae)*		300 500	300 500
25/1/2017	**Received payment from debtors $900 in full settlement** Cash a/c Sales discount a/c To Accounts receivale		900 100	1000

What did we observe?

Transactions	Inventory cost	CGS
Purchase of inventory	Increase	
Transport inward expenses	Increase	
Goods sold	Decrease	Increase
Goods retruned from customer	Increase	Decrease
Goods retruned to the vendors	Decrease	
Transport outward expenses	Unaffected	
Discount received form Vendors	Decrease	
Discount given to customers	Unaffected	

NOTE: For every increase and decrease in inventory cost, 'Inventory a/c' is debited and credited.

Inventory and CGS ledger accounts

Inventory a/c

	Debit		Credit
To Accounts payable	2000	By CGS	1200
To Cash	100	By Accounts payable	500
To CGS	**300**	By Accounts payable	200
		By balance c/d	500
	2400		2400

CGS a/c

	Debit		Credit
To inventory a/c	1200	By inventory a/c	300
		By profit and loss a/c	**900**
	1200		1200

Trail Balance

Trail balance		Debit	Credit
Inventory		500	
CGS		900	
Sales			1500
Delivery expenses		50	
Accounts payable (2000-500-1500)		0	0
Sales return		500	
Sales discount		100	
Accounts receivable(1500-500-1000)		0	
Cash (-100-50-1300+900)			550
(since cash balace is credit it is treated as overdraft a/c)			
		2050	2050

Income statement and Balance sheet

Income statement for the period ended 31-1-2017					
		Debit ($)			Credit ($)
CGS		900	Sales	1500	
			less: Sales return	500	
			Less: Discount on sales	100	
Gross profit		NIL	Net sales		900
		1500			1500
			Gross profit		NIL
Delivery expenses		50			
			Net loss		50
		50			50

Balance Sheet as on 31-1-2017				
Equity and liability			Assets	
Owner's equity			Non-current assets	
Retained earnings	-50			
Current liabilities			Current assets	
Overdraft	550		Inventory	500.00
	500			500.00

Periodic inventory management system

In this system **inventories are counted at the end of a specific period.** Normally the period is one year. Cost of goods sold cannot be determined until the count of inventory is done to identify the closing inventory.

Note: companies using the periodic inventory system for their general ledger often maintain sophisticated inventory systems **outside** of the general ledger for tracking the goods it purchases, produces, sells and has on hand.

Accounting features

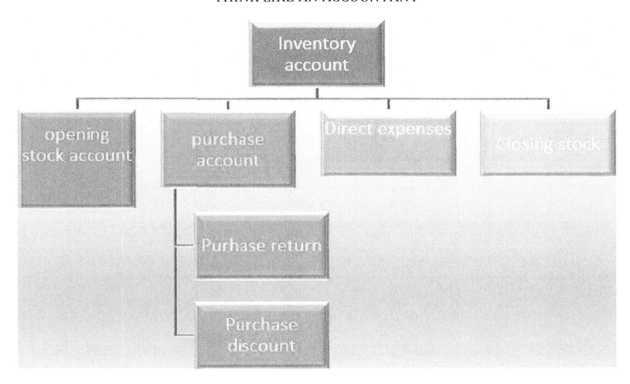

1. Inventory account is broken into four parts:

A. Opening stock account

B. Purchases account—Purchase return account—Purchase discount account

C. Direct expenses account (fright, taxes, insurance etc.)

D. Closing stock account.

2. There is no cost of goods sold account. CGS is calculated by transferring all parts of inventory account to trading account or income statement. CCGS = Opening stock + Purchases + direct expenses – Closing stock.

3. All other account are maintained similar to perpetual inventory system.

4. Closing stock is an adjustment item. It needs to be either adjusted to the purchases account or it can directly adjusted in trading and profit & loss account. Physical count of inventory is done at the period end to determine closing stock quantity. Closing stock cost is determined by any of the cost assignment method (discussed later)

Common Journal entries for periodic inventory system

Example:

1. Jan 1. Purchase goods on credit $2000.

2. Jan 5. Shipping expenses paid to receive goods $ 100

3. Jan 10. Sold goods for credit $1500. Cost of these goods were $1200.

4. Jan 10. Shipping expenses paid for delivery of Goods $50.

5. Jan 12. Return of goods purchased $500.

6. Jan 15. Paid to creditors $1300 (discount received $200).

7. Jan 20. Goods returned from customers priced at $500. Cost of these goods are 300.

8. Jan 25. Received payment from debtors in full settlement $900 (discount given $100)

Note: Full settlement means amount due is settled in full and there is no remaining balance to be paid or received.

Journal

Date	Partiulars			Debit	Credit
1/1/2017	**Purchases of Goods on credit.**				
	Purchases a/c			2000	
	To Accounts payable				2000
5/1/2017	**Shipping expenses paid to receive goods**				
	Shipping expenses a/c			100	
	To Cash				100
10/1/2017	**Sold goods for credit $1500. Cost of these goods are $1200**				
	Cost of goods sold a/c				
	Inventory a/c				
	(This entry is not recorded)				
	Accounts receivable a/c			1500	
	Sales				1500
	(Recording of revenue)				
10/1/2017	**Shipping expenses paid for delivery of goods**				
	Delivery expenses a/c			50	
	Cash a/c				50
12/1/2017	**Return of goods purchased $500**				
	Accounts payable a/c			500	
	Purchase return a/c				500
15/1/2017	**Paid to creditors $1300 in full settlement**				
	Accounts payable a/c			1500	
	To Cash				1300
	To purchase discount a/c				200
20/1/2017	**Goods retutned from customers priced $500. Cost of these goods are $300**				
	Inventory a/c				
	Cost of goods sold a/c				
	(This entry is not recorded)				
	Sales return a/c			500	
	Accounts receivable a/c				500
	(Recording of revenue decresae)				
25/1/2017	**Received payment from debtors $900 in full settlement**				
	Cash a/c			900	
	Sales discount a/c			100	
	To Accounts receivale				1000

Trial balance

Trail balance		
	Debit	Credit
Purchases	2000	
Accounts payable (2000-500-1500)		0
Shipping expenses	100	
Sales		1500
Accounts receivable(1500-500-1000)	0	
Delivery expenses	50	
Purchase return		500
Purchase discount		200
Sales return	500	
Sales discount	100	
Cash (-100-50-1300+900)		550
(since cash balace is credit it is treated as overdraft a/c)		
	2750	2750

Adjustments to be done: Closing stock (at the period end physical count of inventory is done. It reveals a closing stock balance of $500)

You can either prepare an adjusted trial balance by adjusting the closing stock to purchases account. Or you can transfer the closing stock to Income statement directly as shown below.

Income statement and Balance sheet

Income statement for the period ended 31-1-2017				
	Debit ($)			Credit ($)
Purchases	2000	Sales	1500	
Less: purchase return	500	less: Sales return	500	
Less: purchase discount	200	Less: Discount on sales	100	
Net purchases	1300	Net sales		900
Shipping expenses	100	Closing stock		500
Gross profit	NIL			
	1500			1500
		Gross profit		NIL
Delivery expenses	50			
		Net loss		50
	50			50

Balance Sheet as on 31-1-2017			
Equity and liability		**Assets**	
Owner's equity		**Non-current assets**	
Retained earnings	-50		
Current liabilities		**Current assets**	
Overdraft	550	Closing inventory	500.00
	500		500.00

Section 3. Assignment of cost to the inventory

How can we determine the value of CGS and closing inventory?

Inventories are purchased during the year at different points of time. ***The cost of purchase inventories may be different at different points of time.***

Below is the details of inventory position and movements during the year 2017 (January to December)

Details	quantity	Price per unit	Cost
Oopening inventory	2	15	30
Purchase in January	1	10	10
Purchase in June	1	25	25
Purhcase in October	1	20	20
Total inventory available for sale	5		85
Sale in June	3	?	?
Closing inventory	2		?

You can see total inventory available for sale during the year was 5 units. Out of which 3 units have been sold.

Cost of the 3 units sold is our cost of goods sold and cost of 2 units that could not be sold is our closing inventory which will appear in our balance sheet as a current asset.

How can we determine the value of CGS and closing inventory?

There are several methods, out of which three methods are important for discussion.

1. FIFO: It is called First in First Out. As per this method we should **move the cost** from oldest inventories first and then from the recent ones. Please note that "movement of cost" is *independent* from movement of "actual physical units." (It means you can move the **cost** of old inventories by transferring physical units of recent goods)

Applying the FIFO concept to our example:

<u>Cost of Goods sold</u>

Perpetual inventory system: We can see 3 inventories are sold. Cost of 2 inventories are moved from opening inventory as it is the **oldest cost** and cost of 1 inventory is moved from January purchase. CGS = 2*15 + 1*10 = 40. **Note:** *the 3 units which are sold may belong to recent purchase in June but the costs are moved from opening stock and January purchase.*

Periodic inventory system: Under periodic inventory system, first we need to determine the cost of closing inventory. Then by applying the formula: Opening stock + Purchases – Closing stock, we arrive at the value of CGS.

CGS = 0 + 85 -45 (see below) = 40

Cost of closing inventory:

Perpetual inventory system: we know we have 2 unit in hand. Cost for these 2 units should be total cost of inventory available less CGS. Closing inventory = 85 – 40 = 45. This cost of $45 includes one unit of June purchased at 25 another unit of October purchased at 20.

Periodic inventory system: We don't have track of CGS under this method. So we count out inventory at year end. We see we have 2 units left. Since we are following FIFO method, the inventories which are sold should be the oldest and the inventories at the end period should be newest cost. **The recent costs are from October and June purchased at 20 and 25. Closing inventory for 2 units will be 20+25 = 45**

Details	quantity	Price per unit	Cost
Oopening inventory	2	15	30
Purchase in January	1	10	10
Purchase in June	1	25	25
Purhcase in October	1	20	20
Total inventory available for sale	5		85
Sale in June	3	2*15 + 1*10	**40**
Closing inventory	2		**45**

2. LIFO: It is called Last in First Out. As per this method we should **move the cost** from newest inventories first and then from the older ones. Please note that movement of cost is independent from movement of actual physical units.

Applying the LIFO concept to our example:

Cost of Goods sold

Perpetual inventory system: In perpetual inventory system we need not wait until period end to know the value of CGS. We can ascertain the CGS when the sale is done, that is in June. Cost of 1st unit is moved from **June** purchase **as it is the newest cost**, cost of 2nd unit is moved from June purchase and cost of 3rd unit is moved from January purchase. CGS = 1*25 + 1*10 + 1*15 = 50.

Periodic inventory system : Cost of Goods sold is determined at the period end. CGS = OS + Purchases – Closing stock = 0 + 85 – 30 (See below) = $55

Cost of closing inventory:

Perpetual inventory system: we know we have 1 unit in hand **at the end of June.** Cost for this 1 unit should be total cost of inventory available **until June** less CGS. Closing inventory = 65 – 50 = 15. This cost of $15 includes one unit from opening stock. Closing inventory **at the end of December** will be closing inventory of June $15 plus one unit purchased in October at 20, that is 20 +25 = 45.

Periodic inventory system: Since we count the closing inventory at period end (year end in this example), we can consider the newest costs moved out form October. But the approach under this system for LIFO will be to assign the oldest costs to the inventories in hand. So we take the cost from opening stock that is $15 per unit for 2 units and our closing stock value will be $30.

3. Weighted average cost: In this method the weighted average cost of materials is taken to move the cost from inventory to CGS.

Applying the WAC concept to our example:

Cost of Goods sold

Perpetual inventory system: In perpetual inventory system we need not wait until period end to know the value of CGS. We can ascertain the CGS when the sale is done, that is in June.

WAC as of June = Total inventory cost until June / total inventory available for sale until June = 65/4 = 16.25

WAC as of December = 85/5 = 17

CGS for 3 inventories which is sold as of June = 3 * 16.25 = 48.75

CGS for 3 inventories which is sold as of December = 3 * 17 = 51

Periodic inventory system: Cost of Goods sold is determined at the period end. CGS = OS + Purchases – Closing stock = 0 + 85 – 34 (See below) = $51

Cost of closing inventory:

Perpetual inventory system:

Cost of closing inventory at the end of June: 1 * 16.25 = 16.25

Cost of closing inventory at the end of June: 2* 17 = 34

Periodic inventory system:

Cost of closing inventory will be determined by applying the WAC at the end of December that is $17 per unit. Closing stock = 2*17 = 34

You should have noticed that CGS under 3 methods under 2 systems are different. ***This results in different gross profits.***

Conclusion: I have presented here a simple version of inventory accounting. I hope this provides you a basic understanding of inventory systems and methods.

Appendix 4 - Accounts Receivable Adjustments

In this chapter we will discuss some of the important adjustments related to Accounts receivable.

Debtors/Accounts receivable: whenever we sell goods or services **on credit** to customers we create Debtors accounts.

Adjustment 1: Bad debts. This is the amount which is **not** recoverable from customers. Normally we wait until the last day of the period to register the bad debts. Hence bad debts would not have been journalized and would not appear in the Trail balance most of the time.

The journal entry for bad debt:

A. Accounts involved in the transaction: Bad debt and Debtors

B. Bad debt is a loss and Debtor is an asset.

C. There is increase in Bad debt a/c and decrease in Debtors a/c.

D. Increase in Bad debt is debited and decrease in debtors is credited.

Date	Partiulars	Debit	Credit
	Bad debts a/c Debtors a/c	XXX	XXX

Let's understand the concept through an example:

Below is the trial balance as on 31/12/2017 of ABC ltd.

Trail balance		Debit	Credit
Accounts recceivable		50000	
Bad debts		1000	

Adjustments: Further Bad debts $1500.

Observations

1. Bad debts given inside 1000: it means the journal entry for Bad debts is already recorded. Accounts receivable or Debtors account is already reduced by $1000.

2. Further Bad debts given outside the trial balance: It means no Journal entry has been passed yet to record this. **An adjustment entry is needs to be registered now**.

Date	Partiulars		Debit	Credit
31/12/2017	Bad debts a/c Accounts receivable a/c		1500	1500

We have two option to proceed further.

1. Prepare adjusted trial balance. From the adjusted trial balance prepare Profit and loss account and balance sheet.

2. No adjusted trial balance is prepared: The effect of adjusting entry will be directly recorded in profit and loss account and balance sheet. Since Bad debt is a loss it will be recorded in the profit and loss account and Accounts receivable in Balance sheet will be reduced by the bad debts amount ($1500)

Option 1. Prepare adjusted trial balance.

Adjusted Trail balance				
			Debit	Credit
Accounts recceivable (50000-1500) Bad debts (1000+1500)			48500 2500	

Profit & loss account and Balance sheet

Income statement for the period ended 31-1-2017	Debit ($)		Credit ($)
Purchases		Sales	
		Closing stock	
Gross profit			
		Gross profit	
Bad debts	2500		

Balance Sheet as on 31-1-2017			
Equity and liability		Assets	
Owner's equity		Non-current assets	
		Current assets	
		Accounts receivable	48,500

Option 2: No adjusted trial Balance is prepared. Direct adjustment into income statement and Balance sheet.

Income statement for the period ended 31-1-2017					
		Debit [$]			Credit [$]
Purchases			Sales		
Shipping expenses			Closing stock		
Gross profit					
			Gross profit		
Bad debts	1000				
Add: Further Bad debts	1500	2500			

Balance Sheet as on 31-1-2017				
Equity and liability		**Assets**		
Owner's equity		Non-current assets		
		Current assets		
		Accounts receivable	50000	
		Less: Bad debts	1500	48,500

Note: it is preferred to prepare an adjusted trial balance if there are more adjustments at year end.

Adjustment 2: Provision for doubtful debts

In simple words, provision means setting aside some amount to cover expected future losses or expenses. Continuing the example, let's say during 2018 ABC limited observed the payments made by the customers form credit sales. It recognized at least 10% of customers are not paying the amounts. In other words, ABC limited is doubtful about the collections from 10% of customers. It decides to make a provision for doubtful debtors **@10% each year going forward.**

This decision is supported by below accounting principles:

A. principle of conservatism: provide for all possible losses.

B. Matching principle: Since credit sales is recognized in this period, expected losses related to these sales needs to be recognized in this period.

 Note: Provision of doubtful debt is always created on Good debts . Good debts are Accounts receivable less Bad debt.

Below is the unadjusted trial balance of ABC ltd **as on 31-12-2018**

Adjusted Trail balance	Debit	Credit
Accounts recceivable	60000	
Bad debts	2500	

Adjustment:

Further bad debt 1000

Create a provision for doubtful debt @10%

As you know we have two options to proceed further:

Option 1: to create Adjusted Trail balance

Option 2: To make direct adjustments in Income statement and Balance sheet

As you are already aware of the process of creating adjusted trial balance, let's proceed with option 2.

Note: The amount of provision for doubtful debt = Good debt * 10% = (60000 – 1000) * 10% = 5900 (Bad debts given within trial balance is already reduced from Accounts receivable)

Adjusting journal entries

Date	Partiulars	Debit	Credit
31/12/2018	Bad debts a/c To Accounts receivable a/c (Recording furher bad debts)	1000	1000
31/12/2018	Income statement a/c To provsion for doubtful debt	5900	5900

Income statement and Balance sheet as on 31-12-2018

Income statement for the period ended 31-1-2018	Debit ($)			Credit ($)
Purchases			Sales	
Shipping expenses			Closing stock	
Gross profit				
			Gross profit	
Bad debts	2500			
Add: Further Bad debts	1000	3500		
Provsion for doubtful debt		5900		

Balance Sheet as on 31-1-2017				
Equity and liability			**Assets**	
Owner's equity			Non-current assets	
			Current assets	
			Accounts receivable	60000	
			Less: Bad debts	1000	
			Less: provsion for doubtful debt	5900	53,100

To understand further how to the provision for doubtful debts work, let's move to year 2019.

Below is the unadjusted Trial balance **as on 31-12-2019**

Adjusted Trail balance			Debit	Credit
Accounts recceivable			40000	
Provsion for doubtful debts				5900

Adjustments:

Scenario 1.

Bad debts: 3500

Provision for doubtful debtors @10%

Scenario 2.

Bad debts: 1000

Provision for doubtful debtors @10%

Let's proceed with scenario 1

Adjustment entries

Date	Partiulars	Debit	Credit
31/12/2019	Bad debts a/c To Accounts recivable (Bad debt recorded)	3500	3500
31/12/2019	Provsion for bad debt a/c To Bad debt a/c (Bad debt adjsusted against available provsion for DD)	3500	3500
31/12/2019	Income statement a/c To provsion for doubtful debt (provsion for doubt ful debt created)	1250	1250

Note: Balance of Good debt = 40000 -3500 =36500. Closing balance of provision needs to be maintained = Good debt * 10% = 36500 *10% = 3650.

Provision available = opening balance less bad debts = 5900- 3500 = 2400

Provision to be created during the year: provision available less closing balance required = 2400 – 3650 = 1250

Provsion for Doubtful debt a/c			
	Debit		Credit
To Bad debts	3500	By balance b/d	5900
To balance c/d	3650	By profit and loss a/c (provsion for this year)	1250
	7150		7150

Income statement and Balance sheet as on 31-12-2019

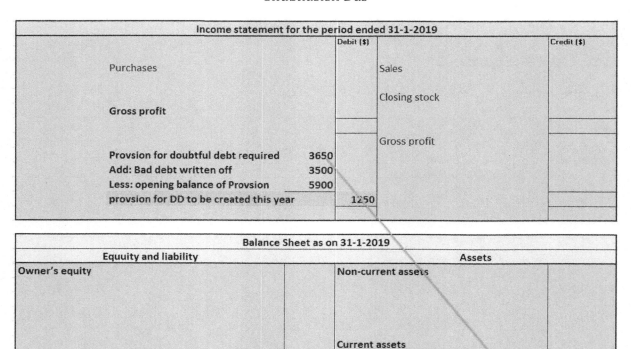

Income statement for the period ended 31-1-2019				
		Debit ($)		Credit ($)
Purchases			Sales	
			Closing stock	
Gross profit				
			Gross profit	
Provsion for doubtful debt required	3650			
Add: Bad debt written off	3500			
Less: opening balance of Provsion	5900			
provsion for DD to be created this year		1250		

Balance Sheet as on 31-1-2019				
Equuity and liability			**Assets**	
Owner's equity			Non-current assets	
			Current assets	
			Accounts receivable	40000	
			Less: Bad debts	3500	
			Less: Provsion for doubtful debt	3650	32,850

Scenario 2.

Adjustment entries

Date	Partiulars	Debit	Credit
31/12/2019	Bad debts a/c To Accounts recivable (Bad debt recorded)	1000	1000
31/12/2019	Provsion for bad debt a/c To Bad debt a/c (Bad debt adjsusted against available provsion for DD)	1000	1000
31/12/2019	Provsion for doubtful debt To income statement (Excess provsion written back)	1000	1000

Note: Balance of Good debt = 40000 -1000 =39000. Closing balance of provision needs to be maintained = Good debt * 10% = 39000 *10% = 3900.

Provision available = opening balance less bad debts = 5900- 1000 = 4900

Excess provision available: 4900 – 3900 = $1000 (This excess provision will be written back to income statement)

Provsion for Doubtful debt a/c				
	Debit			Credit
To Bad debts	1000	By balance b/d		5900
To income statement	1000			
(excess provsion written back)				
To balance c/d	3900			
	5900			5900

Income statement and Balance sheet as on 31-12-2019

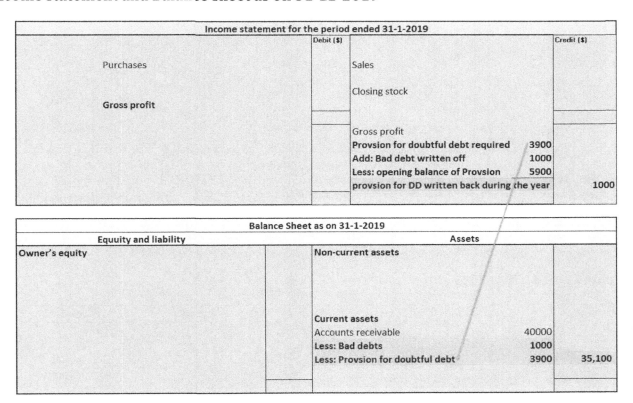

Income statement for the period ended 31-1-2019			
	Debit ($)		Credit ($)
Purchases		Sales	
		Closing stock	
Gross profit			
		Gross profit	
		Provsion for doubtful debt required 3900	
		Add: Bad debt written off 1000	
		Less: opening balance of Provsion 5900	
		provsion for DD written back during the year	1000

Balance Sheet as on 31-1-2019			
Equity and liability		Assets	
Owner's equity		Non-current assets	
		Current assets	
		Accounts receivable 40000	
		Less: Bad debts 1000	
		Less: Provsion for doubtful debt 3900	35,100

Adjustment 3: Provision for discount on debtors

Debtors who pay within the due date may be eligible for some cash discount. At the end of the year, we need to estimate the discount that might be allowed in next year to the Debtors outstanding currently. Since the debt has arisen in this year we need to set aside some amount for the discount that may be allowed on such debts (Matching concept). Hence a provision for discount on debtors needs to be created.

The accounting process is same as provision for doubtful debts.

Note: Provision for discount on debtors always calculated as a % on Good debts. Good debts = Total debtors (-) Bad debts (-) provision for doubtful debts.

Journal entries

Date	Partiulars	Debit	Credit
	Discount allowed a/c To Accounts recivable (For discount allowed to Debtors)	XXX	XXX
	Profit and loss a/c To Discount allowed a/c (Transfering the discount to income statement)	XXX	XXX
	Provsion for dsiscount on debtors a/c To discount allowed a/c (If provision for discount on debtors already exists, then discount is transferred to this account instead of PL a/c)	XXX	XXX
	Profit and loss a/c To provsion for discount on debtors a/c (For creating the provsion for discount on debtors)	XXX	XXX

Example: ABC limited has a Debtors balance of $50000 at 31/12/2017. It decided to create a provision for discount on debtors @5%. It intends to maintain this provision balance each year going forward.

In 2018, actual discount allowed was $3000. Balance of Debtors at 31/12/2018 is $60000.

Journals as on 31/12/2017

Date	Partiulars	Debit	Credit
31/12/2017	Profit and loss a/c To provision for discount on debtors (For creating the provsion for discount on debtors)	2500	2500

Trial balance as on 31/12/2018

Adjusted Trail balance		Debit	Credit
Accounts recceivable		60000	
Provsion for discount on debtors			2500

Adjustments:

1. Discount allowed in 2018 $3000

2. Provision for discount on debtors @ 5%

Adjustment entries

Date	Partiulars	Debit	Credit
31/12/2018	Discount allowed a/c To Debtors a/c (For discount allowed to Debtors)	3000	3000
31/12/2018	Provsion for dsiscount on debtors a/c To discount allowed a/c (For transferring the discount allowed to provsion account)	3000	3000
31/12/2018	Profit and loss a/c To provsion for discount on debtors a/c (For creating the provsion for discount on debtors)	3500	3500

Ledger accounts at 31/12/2018

Provsion on discount on Debtors			
	Debit		Credit
		By Balance b/d	2500
To Discount allowed	3000		
		By profit and loss a/c	3500
To Balance c/d	3000		
	6000		6000
Discount allowed a/c			
	Debit		Credit
To debtors	3000		
		By provsion for DOD	3000
	3000		3000

Note: Provision to be created this year = Provision required to be maintained – provision available.

Provision required to be maintained at 31/12/2018 = 60000 * 5 % = 3000

Provision available at 31/12/2018 = 2500 – 3000 = -500

Provision created during the year = 3000 – (– 500) = 3500

Income statement and Balance sheet

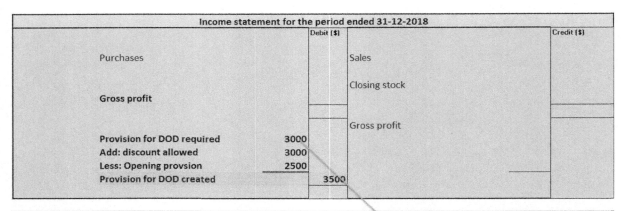

Income statement for the period ended 31-12-2018		Debit ($)			Credit ($)
Purchases			Sales		
			Closing stock		
Gross profit					
			Gross profit		
Provision for DOD required	3000				
Add: discount allowed	3000				
Less: Opening provsion	2500				
Provision for DOD created		3500			

Balance Sheet as on 31-12-2018				
Equity and liability		**Assets**		
Owner's equity		Non-current assets		
		Current assets		
		Accounts receivable	60000	
		Less: Discount allowed	3000	
		Less: Provsion for discount on debtors	3000	54,000

Printed in Great Britain
by Amazon

77092259R00072